On Myself, and Other, Less Important Subjects

D1706362

On Myself, and Other, Less Important Subjects

Caspar John Hare

With an Introduction by Mark Johnston

PRINCETON UNIVERSITY PRESS
Princeton and Oxford

Copyright 2009 © by Princeton University Press

Published by Princeton University Press, 41 William Street, Princeton,
New Jersey 08540
In the United Kingdom: Princeton University Press, 6 Oxford Street, Woodstock,
Oxfordshire OX20 1TR

First paperback printing, 2018
Paper ISBN 978-0-691-17803-5
The Library of Congress has cataloged the cloth edition as follows:

Hare, Caspar John, 1972-
On myself, and other, less important subjects / Caspar John Hare.
    p. cm.
Includes bibliographical references and index.
ISBN 978-0-691-13531-1 (cloth : alk. paper)   1. Self (Philosophy)
2. Solipsism.   I. Title.
    BD450.H287 2009
    126—dc22
    2009001387

British Library Cataloging-in-Publication Data is available

This book has been composed in Minion with Myriad display
Printed on acid-free paper. ∞
press.princeton.edu
Printed in the United States of America

To absent friends

Contents

Contents

Acknowledgments

Time for thanks. Many people have given me a tremendous amount of help with this project. I would like to thank, in particular, Alex Byrne, Bob Stalnaker, Steven Yablo, Agustin Rayo, Simon Keller, and an anonymous reviewer working pro bono for Princeton University Press, for wonderful comments on recent iterations of the manuscript. Special mention goes to Mark Johnston, for helping me to develop the central ideas, and Benj Hellie, for near-heroic line-by-line commentary. Without Mark's encouragement this book would never have existed. Without Benj's interventions it would have been much less good.

Finally, I would like to thank Melissa Mohr. I imagine that it is trying, at the best of times, when your husband squirrels himself away to write a book. But it takes a special kind of mental fortitude to tolerate your husband's squirreling himself away to write a defense of solipsism.

Introduction

The short work you have before you is quite remarkable. Not just for the penetrating clarity of its philosophical prose, and not just for its uncompromising determination to follow the argument wherever it leads.

The work announces that there is someone among us who is absolutely special, who has no peers, or "no neighbors" as Ludwig Wittgenstein once put it, by way of describing solipsism. The character of this person's mental life is graced by a feature— "presence"—found in the mental life of no other.

As it turns out, we readers are particularly fortunate in that the author, Caspar Hare, is ideally well placed to describe the special one whose experiences are the only experiences that are present. For, as it happens, Caspar Hare himself is the special one.

He is not kidding, at least not in any simple way. *On Myself, and Other, Less Important Subjects* is a profoundly serious provocation. It works to deny us any coherent part of logical space in which to locate our commonsense conviction that we are all on a par when it comes to presence. Even if the tongue is sometimes in the cheek, this never interferes with the beautifully continuous line of argument from things we all believe to things all but one of us will find unbelievable.

In setting out this line of argument, *On Myself, and Other, Less Important Subjects* offers the philosophically most sophisticated form of solipsism (from *solus ipse*—oneself alone) that I have encountered. This is not the crude, almost universally rejected, solipsism that denies the existence of other minds. Hare himself insists that distinct functional systems of mental events and states are located in other bodies; so much is the result of any reasonable inference to the best explanation of the behavior of others. This inference to the best explanation of the behavioral evidence is widely regarded as having refuted solipsism. Yet, as Hare's monograph shows, accepting all that is entirely compatible with a deeper and more disturbing solipsism to the effect that the experiences of others are just not present.

Hare offers an engagingly direct illustration of his point. Pour a little boiling water on the back of your hand: Pain is present. But now consider all the unfortunate Russians who, within the last few hours, accidentally did something similar. Their experiences of pain were real, but they were manifestly not present. Search as you might in your memory of what was present in the last hours, the pains associated with all those unfortunate Russian scaldings are not be found.

You will say this is a mighty confusion. "Those pains were not present to *me*, but take any one of the pains, surely it was present to the person whose scalding caused the pain in question." A very natural thing to think; in fact it can seem the only thing to think.

Here it is crucial to realize that Hare is in effect assuming a version of what philosophers have called the "no-self" or "no-ownership" theory, namely, that the presentations of objects and experiences that make up our conscious life are not presentations of objects and experiences *to a subject or self.* David Hume sounded the rallying cry for this conviction when he wrote:

There are some philosophers, who imagine we are every moment intimately conscious of what we call our SELF; that we feel its existence and its continuance in existence; and are certain, beyond the evidence of a demonstration, both of its perfect identity and simplicity. To attempt a farther proof of this were to weaken its evidence; since no proof can be deriv'd from any fact, of which we are so intimately conscious; nor is there any thing, of which we can be certain, if we doubt of this.

For my part, when I enter most intimately into what I call *myself*, I always stumble on some particular perception or other, of heat or cold, light or shade, love or hatred, pain or pleasure. I never can catch *myself* at any time without a perception, and never can observe any thing but the perception. . . . If any one, upon serious and unprejudic'd reflection thinks he has a different notion of *himself*, I must confess I can reason no longer with him. All I can allow him is, that he may be in the right as well as I, and that we are essentially different in this particular. He may, perhaps, perceive something simple and continu'd, which he calls *himself*; tho' I am certain there is no such principle in me.[1]

As I would put it, when we attend to the structure of any conscious act, there is an object of consciousness, be it an external item or an experience, thought, emotion, belief, etc. And there is the manner of presentation of that object. But there is not a third term in the conscious act, the self or subject to whom objects are presenting in that manner. Conscious acts are owned by individual persons only in the sense that they are united in mentally coherent bundles of events and states, bundles contingent on the operation of individual brains and nervous systems. So much is the content of the no-self or no-ownership theory.

Given the theory, the most natural thing to say or think in response to Hare's illustration turns out to be an illegitimate attempt to relativize presence on the subject end. If presence is never presence to someone or other, if objects and experiences are just present *sans phrase*, then the only thing to conclude from reflection on one's own scalding and the scaldings of all those unfortunate Russians is that while one's own pains are present, their pains are not present.

We may usefully compare Hare's point here with one of Wittgenstein's deepest thoughts about other minds, the thought forcefully set out in the unjustly neglected second essay in Saul Kripke's famous *Wittgenstein on Rules and Private Language*. In that essay, "Wittgenstein on Other Minds," Kripke locates something like Hume's no-ownership theory as the source of Wittgenstein's claims that it is no easy thing to conceive of another's pain on the model of one's own, and that attempting to do so may be as conceptually incoherent as talking of time on the sun. How could I generalize an inner presentation like pain from my own case, if it is not a case or an example of something more general, namely, pain presented *to a self*?

This is one source of the so-called conceptual problem of other minds: How am I even so much as in a position to entertain the hypothesis of another's pain, given that my experience of pain is not a presentation to a self that happens to be one self among other selves?

Wittgenstein seems to have regarded the conceptual problem as an upshot of an artificial, Cartesian construal of pain as a purely inner sensation wholly individuated by its qualitative character. Instead, our concept of pain is a concept of an inner state that has characteristic behavioral expressions. To be able to see those behavioral expressions as expressions of pain is part of understanding what pain is, an understanding we rely on even when we attribute pain to ourselves directly and without recourse to our own behavior. So for Wittgenstein, the absence of an owning self for my pains, in Hare's terms the idea that the presence of pain is not presence to a self or subject, does not threaten the idea that others' behavior might express their pain. Indeed, for Wittgenstein, that possibility is already provided for when I attribute pain to myself and do this directly, that is, not on the basis of my own behavior. For what I am attributing to myself is a state with such and such characteristic behavioral expressions.

However, that perfectly correct Wittgensteinian point may not seem to cut deeply enough when it is *presence* itself that is at issue. To make sense of presence is to make sense of something that is conceptually independent of any behavioral manifestation. If we *can* make sense of presence, then something like the argument envisaged by Kripke will remain: Given the no-self theory, imagining experiences present to another on the model of experiences present to me will be "none too easy a thing to do." If, as Hare puts it, presence is a monadic feature applying to certain experiences, then there is no room for the idea of experiences being present *to another*. (Or *to me* for that matter.)

So much the worse, you might say, for the idea of presence—as it were the most abstract distillation of the Cartesian idea of the "innerness" of sensations. Anticipating this sort of reaction, Hare argues that it is very natural to appeal to presence in explaining what is so disconcerting about one's own death. In fearing death we fear the end of presence:

> When I was a child I was gripped by all kinds of quasi-solipsistic fantasies—convinced that the people around me were all aliens or actors or robots or secret agents or whatever. So far so normal. As I grew up so I grew out of this phase, I stopped jumping around doors to catch

the aliens off guard . . . etc., and generally became more mellow. But one quasi-solipsistic thought survived into my adolescence. It would arise most distinctively when I thought about death. What would my death be like? I would imagine a vicious internal cramp as my heart gives out, panic and fear as my muscles become limp and then, as the blood stagnates in my head and my brain starves of oxygen . . . what? My school vicar said *light*. Homer, in a much more impressive way, said *darkness*:

> Achilles smote him with his sword and killed him. He struck him in the belly near the navel, so that all his bowels came gushing out on to the ground, and the darkness of death came over him as he lay gasping.[2]

> The sword reeked with his blood, while dark death and the strong hand of fate gripped him and closed his eyes. Idomeneus speared Erymas in the mouth; the bronze point of the spear went clean through it beneath the brain, crashing in among the white bones and smashing them up. His teeth were all of them knocked out and the blood came gushing in a stream from both his eyes; it also came gurgling up from his mouth and nostrils, and the darkness of death enfolded him round about.[3]

But even then I understood that neither was right. After my death there would be a kind of *nothingness*, a kind of *absence* that was difficult to describe or imagine. The closest I could come to picking it out with words was by appeal to precedent—things would be the way they were before I was born. But now I was struck by a thought. Isn't it amazing and weird that for millions of years, generation after generation of sentient creatures came into being and died, came into being and died, and all the while there was this absence, and then one creature, CJH, unexceptional in all physical and psychological respects, came into being, and POW! Suddenly there were present experiences!

Was I thinking about presence and absence in a relational sense? Clearly not, for there is nothing at all amazing or weird about the fact that for millions of years sentient creatures existed without any experiences being present to CJH, and then CJH was born and suddenly experiences were present to CJH. To the extent that I found it amazing and weird that CJH's birth brought an end to millions of years of absence, I must have been thinking about presence and absence in the monadic sense.[4]

Hare's view is that his experiences are present. *Period.* The best that can be said for others is that from their respective points of view, experiences are present (one of Hare's main projects is to offer a way of making sense of this idea—that from other people's points of view other experiences are present—without thinking of presence as a relational property; see sections 3.2–3.4). Hare therefore thinks of himself as the one to whom experiences are present *period*, and whether those experiences are bad or good is important, important *period.*

He expects us all to resonate with this; each of us extends to himself or herself a special metaphysical privilege, not the privilege of being the only mind; obviously others have minds, experiences and external items that are present from their point of view. Each takes himself or herself to be the one to whom experiences and external items are simply present. As mentioned earlier, Hare invites us to try the following little thought experiment:

> ***Trial by Kettle*** | Today, many hundreds, if not thousands, of Russians will spill boiling water on their hands. Pour boiling water on your own hand and compare your present discomfort with the absent discomfort of the northern-most Russian spiller. Which is worse?

Your immediate reaction, "This pain is dreadful, far worse than anything that is going on in Russia" may be tempered by a sober, reflective thought:

> "My pain appears worse to me because I am more intimately acquainted with it. It is present to me in a way that the northern-most Russian spiller's pain is not. But he is more intimately acquainted with his pain. It is present to him in a way that mine is not. Since our situations are really symmetrical, I find, on reflection, that

I have no grounds for thinking that my pain is worse simpliciter than his pain."

Well and good. But this humbling thought is not available. . . . It's not that my pain is present to me and his present to him. Mine is present and his is absent. That is part of the way things are. So there is no reason to qualify or reassess my initial judgment.

Of course . . .

Hare continues,

I will take it that our situations do have something important in common—the northern-most Russian spiller is not a zombie, so just as it is the case that *from CJH's point of view* (there is excruciating pain), so *from the northern-most Russian spiller's point of view* (there is excruciating pain). . . . The way that *from another person's point of view* (. . . things are) matters. That is why empathy is instructive . . . empathizing with an unfortunate involves imagining that I am the unfortunate, that the unfortunate has present experiences. This involves viscerally imagining what *from the unfortunate's point of view* (. . . is the case). And I care about the results of this exercise because I care about *what from another person's point of view* (. . . is the case) . . . . I do not regard presence as an enabling condition for experiences to matter, but as a kind of *factor,* that makes certain pleasures better and certain sufferings worse.[5]

In this way, Hare is able to carry out his main theoretical ambition, which is to align the Consequentialist idea that the only things that matter are states of the world with the natural egocentric idea that one's own experiences, say of pleasure and pain, matter more than the experiences of others. One aspect of a total state of the world is a specification of just whose experiences are present!

Well then, let us begin to specify the total state of the world, and answer who it is that is the one whose experiences are present? Hare answers that it is a manifest fact that the one is, and always has been, Caspar Hare.

This is, of course, an obvious mistake. If there is *one* to whom experiences (and external items) are present then that one, I can assure you, is Mark Johnston. As Hare's advisor, I alerted him to this manifest fact time and time again, but somehow, despite my very considerable persuasive powers, he would always fall back into thinking that he was *the one*, the one to whom experiences and external items are present, thereby denying a manifest fact.

At Hare's dissertation defense (this book grew out of ideas in his dissertation) the question arose among the examiners as to whether a thesis, however brilliant, could be passed if it denied a manifest fact. We all agreed this was a problem, but we had a worse problem: We could not agree on just *which* manifest fact it did deny. Depressingly, it emerged that each examiner thought he was the one whose experiences are present. Seeing these other examiners also deny the manifest fact, namely, the fact that I am the one, it seemed to me unfair to hold the candidate to a higher standard. And, of course, each of the examiners had his own version of that thought. So we had to pass Hare, even though we all believed he had denied a manifest fact!

(I should mention that the examiners may have been a little confused. The author does not ask of anyone else that he or she believe that Caspar Hare is the one with present experiences. He grants—it is indeed part of his view—that I should believe that Mark Johnston is the one with present experiences, and that you should believe that you are the one whose experiences are present. We each may be grateful for that, but I suspect that we may also want something more.)

Joking aside, there is something to the idea that the examiners' predicament is the general predicament. There is something about the structure of self-consciousness that invites each of us to grant ourself a special metaphysical and practical privilege, namely, to indulge in a refined sort of solipsism and in a corresponding practical egocentrism.

The striking achievement of Hare's work is to have made this general predicament so philosophically vivid.

Mark Johnston

On Myself, and Other, Less Important Subjects

1 Self-Interest and Self-Importance

It is common to have a mildly exaggerated sense of the significance of your own joys and miseries, but *grand* self-importance is rare. Louis XIV was grandly self-important. He believed that, when he consumed too much foie gras, *France* suffered gastric pain. When he took satisfaction from the construction of a new fountain on the grounds of Versailles, that feeling would settle over his natural kingdom—from the docks of Brest to the pox-ridden slums of Marseilles. For Louis, self-indulgence was a *national mission.*

> When we have the state in mind, we are working for ourselves. The welfare of the one creates the glory of the other. When the former is happy, lofty and powerful, he who is the cause of it has glory too and consequently should enjoy more than his subjects with regard to himself and to them everything in life that is most pleasant.[1]

We, the undistinguished masses, are not as fortunate as Louis. As one of the masses, I know I have a set of unique qualities—a unique height, a unique weight, a unique time and place of origin, etc., but these give me scarce grounds for thinking that I occupy a special place in the larger scheme of things, that my pleasures and pains are more significant than anybody else's. I am not the physical embodiment of a national spirit. No God has chosen me as his special representative on Earth. I am hardly stronger, faster, or more delicate than the next person. And there are *seven billion* next people.

This means that, though I may be no less chronically attentive to my own comfort than Louis was, my self-attention is internally vexed in a way that his was not. Louis took his pleasures and pains to be especially important, so when he deliberated he discovered a pleasing harmony between *egocentric-hedonistic considerations* (of the form: 'over all, I will suffer less if I do ____ rather than ____') and *considerations of the greater good* (of the form: 'over all, things will be better if I do ____ rather than ____'). When I deliberate I discover no such harmony. I am continually faced with situations in which these considerations conflict, situations in which I can make the world better at a cost to my comfort, and myself more comfortable at cost to the world.

This may seem a very obvious observation. Of course we are, most of us, chronically preoccupied with our own comfort. Of course, to be so preoccupied is not to be preoccupied with the greater good.

Can it be denied?

1.1 Conflicting Considerations

To get a more precise grip on this question, let us consider the position of someone, call her a *peacemaker*, whose desire for the kind of psychological harmony enjoyed by Louis leads her to be resolutely committed to the view that, for the most part, there is no conflict between egocentric-hedonistic considerations and considerations of the greater good.

This peacemaker notes, first, that although most of us are not *extreme egocentric hedonists*, caring about only our own pleasures and pains, we are at least *mild egocentric hedonists*. All other things being equal, we prefer that pain befall others rather than ourselves and pleasure befall ourselves rather than others.

If you are outraged by this suggestion, imagine learning that a hundred thousand people will suffer painful epileptic seizures tomorrow. This will, I guess, trouble you very little. Around a hundred thousand people suffer painful epileptic seizures every day. Now imagine learning that you are among the hundred thousand. This will, I guess, trouble you a good deal. And you will wish it were not so.

Never fear. The peacemaker then claims:

(Harmony)   Whenever a mild egocentric hedonist favors a situation in which she suffers less, she thereby favors a simply better maximal state of affairs.

I have used some quasi-technical terms here, and they need to be glossed. What is it to for one thing to be "simply better" than another? Let us just say what it is not—not better in some qualified or three-way relational sense of the word, not better *for me*, or better *for some purpose*, or better *in relation to a particular set of interests*, but better *period*.

What is a "state of affairs"? Think of a state of affairs as a way for things to be. So the way things in Yosemite National Park are is a state of affairs. The way things in the Russian economy are is a state of affairs. What is a "maximal state of affairs"? It is, first, a way for *everything* to be—if some things are this way, then there are no further things. And it is, second, a *fully specified way* for everything to be—if some things are this way, then there is no further way they might or might not be.

Finally, what is it to "favor a situation"? I mean the notion of "favoring" to be understood quite broadly: One way to favor a situation is bring it about; another is just to desire that it obtain. So, according to (Harmony), it is not just that the actions of a mild egocentric hedonist bring about the good (whenever she brings about a situation in which she suffers less, she brings about a better maximal state of affairs), it is also that the desires of a mild egocentric hedonist align with the good (whenever she wants a situation in which she suffers less to come about, she wants a better maximal state of affairs to come about.)

Is (Harmony) credible? Well, three seemingly insurmountable obstacles stand in the way of my believing it.

The Grounding Problem

First, if I am to believe it, then it must be true of *me* that when I enhance my own comfort at the expense of other people, I am making for a better maximal state of affairs. So I must adopt a picture of the world according to which my comfort makes an especially weighty contribution to the value simpliciter of maximal states of affairs. Call this the *Grounding Problem*: My picture of who I am, and of how I fit into the world, must somehow give me grounds for thinking that my pains and pleasures have an especially important place in the larger scheme of things.

But how can this be? I am not the Sun-King. I am ordinary in all measurable respects. So perhaps my only hope is to believe I am extraordinary in some immeasurable respect, that I am metaphysically unique in some way that bears on the value of my suffering—perhaps I am a God, perhaps I am dreaming up the world, or perhaps I am a solitary utility monster, loose among the unsuspecting masses.

> **The Solitary Utility Monster** | My physiology is not unusual in any measurable way—I wince when punched, smile when pleased, and frown when saddened, just like anyone else. But there is one important, hidden difference between me and other people: My experiences are qualitatively far more intense than theirs. If their experiences are like watercolors by Joseph Turner, mine are like oil paintings by Francis Bacon. Drinking tea feels to me just the way taking morphine feels to them. A touch of indigestion feels to me just the way being disemboweled feels to them.

What if this were true of me? It is a bleak thought. Beyond my immediate horizons, things are dull. My feelings of love and compassion are only faintly reciprocated. My generosity causes little pleasure, my spite little pain. The world is, in a certain sense, unresponsive to me. Perhaps the only consolation would be my blissful ignorance. It is hard to imagine evidence that would count for or against this picture, so only a desperately self-interested person would suspect the awful truth.

But if I were a solitary utility monster, then one might argue that I *should* be self-interested. One might argue that my pleasures and pains would be intrinsically more important than everybody else's. For surely what is intrinsically good or bad about pleasure or pain is its phenomenal aspect. Hit your hand hard against your desk. What is bad about pain is *that* feeling. Run your fingers gently across your scalp. What is good about pleasure is *that* feeling. And there are more of those sorts of feelings associated with my experiences than with anybody else's.

So the solitary utility monster picture would do a fine job of grounding self-interest on my part. But it is, of course, ridiculous. Serious philosophers do not believe they are metaphysically unique. At best they use the idea as a foil—the *problem* of the "problem of other minds" is almost always taken to be the problem of how one can know that other people's mental states are just like one's own, very rarely taken to be the problem of *whether* other people's mental states are just like one's own. And to my knowledge, no serious philosopher has ever even considered the view that I, Caspar Hare, am metaphysically unique. It has not even been in the ballpark!

So this does not seem like a very promising strategy. If I am to solve the Grounding Problem, I must do so without committing myself to a wildly implausible metaphysical picture. And that appears impossible.

The Generalization Problem

Furthermore, if I am to argue, quite generally, that there is no conflict between the considerations that move a mild egocentric hedonist and considerations of the greater good, it is not enough just to show that there is no conflict in my own case. I must show that *any* mild egocentric hedonist, in favoring situations in which she suffers less, is favoring better maximal states of affairs. And it is very difficult to see how this can be so. Call this the *Generalization Problem*.

The central difficulty is illustrated by a famous argument against ethical egoism, in G. E. Moore's *Principia Ethica*. Moore, for reasons that do not concern us here, endorsed a strong consequentialist constraint on reasons and argued, from this assumption, that ethical egoism must be false.

> The only reason I can have for aiming at 'my own good' is that it is good absolutely that what I so call should belong to me—good absolutely that I should have something, which, if I have it, others cannot have. But if it is good absolutely that I should have it, then everyone else has as much reason for aiming at my having it, as I have myself. If, therefore, it is true of any man's 'single interest' or 'happiness' that it ought to be his sole, ultimate end, this can only mean that that man's 'interest' or 'happiness' is the sole good, the universal good, and the only thing that anybody ought to aim at. What Egoism holds, therefore, is that each man's happiness is the sole good—that a number of different things are each of them the only good thing there is—an absolute contradiction! No more complete and thorough refutation of a theory could be desired.[2]

To see Moore's thought, imagine a situation where my interests are at odds with someone else's. For example:

> **Competing for a Scarce Resource** | Jane and I are competing for a scarce resource. It is better for Jane that she get it, and better for me that I get it.

In this situation there seem to be two ways everything might be:

Way (1)	CJH gets the resource and is content	Jane misses out and is miserable

Way (2)	CJH misses out and is miserable	Jane gets the resource and is content

Being an egoist, I favor Way (1) over Way (2). Being an egoist, Jane favors Way (2) over Way (1). But it cannot both be better simpliciter that things be Way (1) and better simpliciter that things be Way (2). So surely in this case at least one of us, in favoring what is better for ourselves, is not favoring a simply better maximal state of affairs. So, for at least one of us, egocentric-hedonistic considerations do not align with considerations of the greater good. If I am to believe the peacemaker, I must somehow find grounds for denying this.

The Problem of Irreducibly Egocentric Preferences

The third problem arises from the fact that, for me, caring about CJH and caring about *me* do not always amount to the same thing. Given that I am broadly egocentric and that I believe myself to be CJH, I want to promote my well-being and the well-being of CJH. But, given that I am broadly egocentric, the moment I ceased to believe I was CJH, I would cease to care about *him* and continue to care about *me*. Here is the kind of situation in which this might happen:

> **After the Train-Crash** | I wake up in hospital, achy and bewildered, unable to remember who or where I am. I try to move and find that my body is swathed in rigid plaster and my head is locked in

a brace. I call for help and receive no reply. But, happily, some kind nurse has placed a television directly in front of me. From it I learn that there has been a terrible train accident, that only two survivors, CJH and Joe Bloggs, have been prised from the wreckage, and that both have been taken to the hospital and placed in full-body plaster casts. "Interesting!" I think, "I must be either CJH or Joe Bloggs." The television then tells me a great deal about the conditions of CJH and Joe Bloggs—CJH is physically like so …, while Joe Bloggs is physically like so …; CJH has such and such a biographical history …, while Joe Bloggs has such and such a biographical history …; they are in adjacent rooms, CJH to the north and Joe Bloggs to the south, but both rooms have a west-facing window; they are both watching television right now, etc. "Interesting!" I think, "I now have an extremely vivid picture of what's going on in this hospital, and I know a tremendous amount about CJH and Joe Bloggs, although I still don't know which of them I am." Finally, the television tells me that one of the two is scheduled to have an extremely long and painful operation in a few hours time. "Interesting!" I think, "I hope that's not *me*."

My first concern in this situation, is for me, not CJH. If I were to discover that CJH was to be the unfortunate subject of the operation, I would be neither happy nor unhappy, because two importantly different possible scenarios would remain open, scenarios that we can represent like this:

| Scenario (1): | CJH suffers | Joe Bloggs is comfortable |
| | | ↑ And this is *me* |

| Scenario (2): | CJH suffers | Joe Bloggs is comfortable |
| | ↑ And this is *me* | |

I very much want the first scenario to obtain. I want to be Joe Bloggs, the person who will not be suffering.

But surely this is a clear example of a mild egocentric hedonist favoring a scenario in which he suffers less without thereby favoring a better maximal state of affairs. For there are not distinct maximal states of affairs corresponding to scenarios (1) and (2). A maximal state of affairs is a fully specified way for everything to be. But it would appear that all the same things exist in scenarios (1) and (2)—both scenarios involve Joe Bloggs, CJH, the television, and so on. And it would appear that all those things are just the same way in both scenarios—Joe Bloggs has a blemish on his right earlobe, CJH's earlobes are perfectly formed, the television is mounted high on a wall, and so on.

If I am to believe the peacemaker, I must somehow find grounds for denying this. I must somehow find grounds for saying that when a mild egocentric hedonist favors Scenario (1) over Scenario (2), he or she is thereby favoring a better maximal state of affairs. But it is very hard to see how this can be so.

1.2 The Way Forward

In light of the Grounding, Generalization, and Irreducibly Egocentric Preferences problems, you may think that the peacemaker's project is hopeless. You may think that the pressing question for ethicists to address is not *whether* the considerations that move a mild egocentric hedonist misalign with considerations of the greater good, but how we should respond *when they do*. And sure enough, ethicists have been responding to some form or other of this question for a very long time.

This may seem like a compelling argument. But it relies on a substantive and questionable metaphysical picture of what the world is like and of how the self fits into the world. If a different picture is right, then the peacemaker's prospects are not so bleak. My aim over the coming chapters is to develop and defend this different picture.

Chapter two is a warm-up. I show that, by adopting an appropriate metaphysical picture, a peacemaker can align time-biased considerations with considerations of the greater good. Chapter three is the main event. By adopting an analogous picture, a picture I call *egocentric presentism*, a peacemaker can align egocentric considerations with considerations of the greater good. In Chapter four I draw some detail into the egocentric presentist picture. In Chapters five and six I argue that it can make sense of some otherwise perplexing matters to do with personal identity over time.

2 Time-Bias and the Metaphysics of Time

Some people care not only about *what* things happen, but also about *when* things happen. One way to care about the when as well as the what is to care about how events are ordered over the course of history—a history across which good and bad things are evenly sprinkled, for example, might seem preferable to one with good things clumped at one end, bad things clumped at the other.[1] Another way is to care more about what happens at some times than others—what happens on the first day of the year 2000, for example, might seem to matter more than what happens on the 326th day of the year 1994. Another way is to care about when things happen relative to the present moment. Call someone who cares about when things happen relative to the present moment *time-biased*.

Of the many ways in which one might be time-biased, the two that have received most attention from philosophers[2] are *hedonic bias toward the future* (all things considered, I prefer that pains be past rather than future and pleasures be future rather than past) and *hedonic bias toward the near* (all things considered, I prefer that pains be in the distant future rather than the immediate future and pleasures be in the immediate future rather than the distant future). All of us seem to be, to some extent, vulnerable to these kinds of bias. We may not take our time-bias to extremes. We may not prefer, for example, that any amount of pain be in the past rather than that any amount of pain be in the future. But we are at least mildly time-biased. We prefer, all other things being equal, that pain be past rather future, far future rather than near future. Would you not prefer to be walking out of your dentist's office, with the pain in your tooth subsiding, than to be walking in, with the bulk of the pain still to come? Would you not prefer the drill to be a week, rather than an hour away?

Let us restrict our attention to pain. Someone who has these sorts of biases may give them a role in her practical reasoning by taking *time-biased hedonistic considerations* (of the form: "there is less future pain in ____ than in ____" or "the future pain in ____ is more distant than in ____") to support favoring one scenario over another. But obviously it would be hasty to take such considerations to provide the last word in practical deliberation, because sometimes they will misalign or conflict with considerations of the greater good. Sometimes, when you desire, or make it the case, that there is less future or near-future pain, you do not desire, or make it the case, that things overall are better.

But why is this so obvious? Once again it will be useful to consider a sort of peacemaker, one whose desire for a harmonious inner life inclines her to think that the considerations that move a mildly time-biased person align with considerations of the greater good. She wants to believe:

> (Harmony II)   Whenever a mildly time-biased person favors a scenario in which there is less future, or near-future pain, she thereby favors a simply better maximal state of affairs.

But can she really manage it? Three familiar obstacles stand in her way:

The Grounding Problem

First, she would have to adopt a metaphysical picture that gave her some grounds for thinking that future pains are in themselves worse than past pains, near-future pains in themselves worse than far-future pains. Her picture would somehow need to give her grounds for thinking, for example, that the suffering of the fallen in the last world war matters less than the suffering of the fallen in the next one. But how can this be? Bullets ripping through flesh in the twentieth century caused no less trauma than bullets ripping through flesh in the twenty-first. It does not seem as if future suffering is measurably different from past suffering. If it is to matter more, then it must be immeasurably different. Here is the sort of picture she would need:

> *Divine Novocain* | At the dawn of creation God faced a problem: He would not allow himself physically to intervene in the course of history, for fear of compromising our freedom, but he wished to

protect us from the evil consequences of that freedom. So he created *divine Novocain*, a drug that dulls the qualitative aspect of suffering without inducing any physical changes in the sufferer. In the past he has administered this drug liberally, to all sufferers, pure and fallen, but now (confronted with famine, war, and pestilence on a scale that even he could not have anticipated) he finds his stocks to be running low. He will be forced to ration. So he decides to administer none for a short while and then gradually build up the doses, though never to their pre-2008 level.

This would do the trick. But it is mad.

The Generalization Problem

Second, it is not enough for our peacemaker to show that considerations of the greater good align with time-biased considerations now, in 2009. She needs to show that they always do. So she needs to deal with cases where time-bias leads us to have conflicting preferences at different times. Here is an example of such a case, where the preferences are generated by bias toward the future.[3]

Bad and Worse Operations | On Monday, doctors run some tests on me and declare that, depending on the results of these tests, I will either have to endure an unpleasant operation on —Thursday or a nightmarish, exquisitely dreadful operation on Tuesday—an operation that involves poking optic fibers down major blood vessels, slicing through muscle tissue, and cauterizing internal wounds with a red-hot scalpel, without so much as an aspirin to distract me from the pain. Not to worry, though; both operations, if performed, will undoubtedly be successful. On Monday I hope to have the unpleasant operation on Thursday. But on Wednesday evening I wake up, bewildered, unable to remember if I have yet been operated on, and, since I am biased toward the future, I very much hope to have had the nightmarish operation on Tuesday.

Here the possible ways that world history might go seem to be:

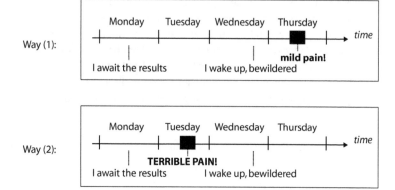

On Monday I prefer (1) to (2), whereas on Wednesday I prefer (2) to (1), consistent with the considerations provided by the Future-Bias Principle. But it cannot both be better that the maximal state of affairs represented by (1) obtain and better that the maximal state of affairs represented by (2) obtain. So on at least one of the two days considerations of the greater good do not align with time-biased hedonistic considerations. On at least one of the two days, in favoring a scenario in which there is less future pain, I am not favoring a better maximal state of affairs.

The Problem of Irreducibly Now-centric Preferences

Third, the peacemaker must face cases where time-bias leads us to have irreducibly now-centric preferences. Here is an example of such a case, where the preference is generated by bias toward the near:[4]

> *Waiting for My Painful Operation* | Early in my life, clever doctors find that I have a rare genetic condition that will most likely cause me to contract cancer of the x (take "x" to refer to whatever organ you feel most anxious about) in late middle age. Happily, they can eliminate the risk by removing organ x from my body. Unhappily, the necessary operation is agonizingly painful. Knowing all this, I

schedule such an operation for soon after April 8, 2022, my fiftieth birthday. I am always perfectly sure that the operation will take place, that I will survive it, that it will be successful, and that it will hurt like anything. Then, one night, I wake up from a fretful dream and look at the date on my malfunctioning alarm clock. It says "April 7,…2." Is it April 7, 2012, or April 7, 2022? For the moment I just do not know. But I do know what I want. Being biased toward the near, I want it to be 2012.

In this case there seem to me to be two possible scenarios:

Scenario (1):

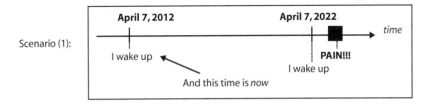

Scenario (2):

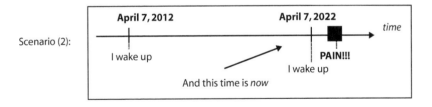

I want the first to obtain, thereby, surely, providing another example of a mildly time-biased person favoring one scenario over another without thereby favoring a better maximal state of affairs. A maximal state of affairs is a fully specified way for everything to be. There cannot be distinct maximal states of affairs corresponding to (1) and (2), because they represent exactly the same fully specified way for world history to be—everything that takes place in the one takes place in the other and in just the same way.

As before, it may appear as if these problems are insurmountable, so it may seem that the peacemaker must give up and concede that no plausible metaphysical picture grounds general time-bias. Time-biased considerations do not always align with considerations of the greater good.

2.1 The Peacemaker's Response

The argument above is structurally just like the argument from chapter one, the argument that egocentric considerations do not always align with considerations of the greater good. Is there anything wrong with it? Well, this time around we have at least some reason to suspect that there might be something wrong with it, because its conclusion is at least controversial. Certainly, many influential philosophers (including Sidgwick[5] and Rawls[6]) have had a low view of time-bias, arguing that it is petty, unenlightened, or, in the extreme, irrational, but many others (including Bentham[7]) have thought it to be perfectly rational and, furthermore, a bias toward what is *better full stop*. It is better full stop that, for example, suffering be in the past rather than the future.

One way to accommodate this intuition would be to take issue with my characterization of the sorts of states of affairs whose value gives rise to considerations of the greater good. I took them to be maximal states of affairs, but one could perhaps take them to be nonmaximal states of affairs—ways for future things to be, perhaps. In favoring better futures I may, then, be favoring better "states of affairs" of the relevant kind (Lars Bergstrom once endorsed this view, arguing that, for consequentialists, "the future is more important than the total state of the world."[8]) Or, for a quite general solution to problems of agent and time-bias, one could stipulate that the relevant "states of affairs" are $<world, agent, time>$ triples.[9] It may be the case that (e.g.), in always favoring better futures, I am always favoring better "states of affairs" in this sense, because it may be that whenever $<w_1, a_1, t_1>$ and $<w_2, a_2, t_2>$ are such that there is less suffering in w_1 after t_1 than in w_2 after t_2, then $<w_1, a_1, t_1>$ is simply better than $<w_2, a_2, t_2>$.

But there is something fishy about this suggestion. For one thing, notice that there is negligible difference between saying that the triple $<w, a_1, t_1>$ is simply better than the triple $<w, a_2, t_2>$, and saying that world w is better for, or in relation to, a_1 at t_1 than for, or in relation to a_2 at t_2. For another thing, it mischaracterizes the nature of the considerations in question. Considerations of the greater good gain their force from the thought that what matters is the way everything is, not the way everything is relative to a time, place, or person. But the triples $<w, a_1, t_1>$

and $<w, a_2, t_2>$ do not represent different ways for everything to be.

Another, much better way to accommodate the intuition is to question whether facts about which time is *now* do not somehow enter into the way everything is. This involves making some substantive assumptions about the metaphysics of time.

Four-Dimensionalism

One important question in the metaphysics of time concerns the ontological status of past, present, and future moments, events, objects. What sorts of entities exist? Does Julius Caesar exist? Does the ninetieth President of the United States exist?

Call someone who believes that past and future entities (moments, events, objects, etc.) exist an *eternalist*. Some eternalists are *ersatz realists* about the past and future; they believe that present things are concrete, past and future things abstract. Others believe that past, present, and future things are equally concrete. "The world consists of a four-dimensionally extended space-time manifold," these people say, "the past, present, and future are ontologically on a par. Just as a thing is no less concrete for being to my left or right, so a thing is no less concrete for coming before or after me." Call such people *block-universe theorists*.

Another important question concerns the status of tensed properties. Think of a property as a way for a thing to be. One way, you might think, for a thing to be is for it to be past. For example, Harold's death at Hastings is past. What is it for a thing to be this way? And what is for a thing to be present? And what is it for a thing to be future?

Some ways for a thing to be past, present, and future are such that being these ways involves standing in some relation to something. For example:

(R1)   Being past relative to Ann Boleyn's death at the Tower.

(R2)   Being present relative to William's invasion of Britain.

(R3)   Being future relative to Jesus' death at Golgotha.

Harold's death at Hastings would appear to have R1, because it precedes Ann Boleyn's death at the Tower, and R2, because it is contemporaneous with William's invasion of Britain, and R3, because it succeeds Jesus' death at Golgotha. Call these *relational tensed properties*. If there are any relational tensed properties, there are many, many of them.[10]

Other ways for a thing to be past, present and future are not such that being these ways involves standing in some relation to something. For example:

(M1)   Being past.

(M2)   Being present.

(M3)   Being future.

Harold's death at Hastings would appear to have M1, but not M2 or M3. Call these *monadic tensed properties*. If there are any monadic tensed properties, there are fewer of them.

Four-dimensionalists are block-universe theorists who believe that there are relational tensed properties but no monadic tensed properties.[11] "All things are on a par with respect to tense," these people say, "all things are future relative to things that come before them, present relative to things with which they coexist, and past relative to things that come after them. No moment has the privileged status of being the present one."

If we accept four-dimensionalism, then the temporal versions of the Grounding, Generalization, and Irreducibly Now-centric Preferences problems really are insoluble. With respect to grounding, past pains are just as real as future pains, so we have no grounds for thinking them less important simpliciter. With respect to generalization, in the "bad and worse operations" case, my preferences between maximal states of affairs do indeed switch between Monday and Wednesday. On Monday I favor the one uncentered space-time manifold over the other, while on Wednesday I favor the other over the one, so I cannot, on both days, be favoring better ways for everything to be. With respect to now-centric preferences, in the "waiting for my painful operation" case, the scenarios that seem open to me indeed do not correspond to distinct maximal states of affairs. When I desire that my pain be in the far future rather than the near future, I am not favoring one uncentered space-time manifold over another, not favoring a better over a worse way for everything to be.

So if we accept four-dimensionalism, then the argument goes through—considerations of the greater good do not always align with time-biased considerations. But what if we reject it? What if we reject the block-universe ontology or concede that there are monadic tensed properties? What if we think that tense is built into the way the world is?

Alternatives to Four-Dimensionalism

There are several ways to accommodate this basic thought. Advocates of the "moving spotlight theory" retain the block-universe ontology, retain the idea that the world is a four-dimensionally extended space-time manifold, but say that one moment has the interesting monadic property of *being the present one*.[12] Which moment? Well, that changes as time goes by (think of the spotlight moving remorselessly along the block). Others reject the block-universe ontology. Some imagine that the past exists but the future does not. The present is the outermost skin of a block that expands as time goes by.[13] Some imagine that the future exists but the past does not. The present is the outermost skin of a block that contracts as time goes by.[14] Some imagine that the present is the first point at which multiple branches split off from the bare tree trunk of the past.[15] Presentists, meanwhile, hold that only present objects, events, moments exist (and perhaps things that exist timelessly, like gods and numbers).[16] There are no past or future things. The best we can say is that it used to be the case that they existed, or it will be the case that they exist.

Each of these is a theory about the nature and extent of all that there is, where "all" is understood in an unrestricted sense—a theory of what the maximal state of affairs (and its nearby possible neighbors) is like. And, according to each of them, one feature of the maximal state of affairs is that present things are different from past and future things. So, according to each of them, the Generalization and Irreducibly Now-centric Preferences problems do not arise. With respect to generalization, in the "bad and worse operations," case the maximal states of affairs that I discriminate between on Monday (one in which mild pain is in the far future and one in which terrible pain is in the near future) are not the same as the maximal states of affairs that I discriminate between on Wednesday (one in which terrible pain is in the past and one in which mild pain is in the near future), so it is quite possible that on both days I am favoring a simply better maximal state of affairs. With respect to irreducibly now-centric preferences, in the "waiting for the painful operation" case, the two scenarios that seem open to me correspond to different maximal states of affairs (in the one case a maximal state of affairs in which pain is in the far future, in the other a maximal state of affairs in which pain is in the near future), so it is quite possible that, in favoring one scenario over another I am favoring a simply better maximal state of affairs.

So, if a dedicated peacemaker rejects four-dimensionalism, then she can solve the Generalization and Now-centric Preferences problems by stipulating that, all other things being equal, states of affairs in which pain will occur are worse than states of affairs in which pain has occurred, and states of affairs in which pain will happen soon are worse than states of affairs in which pain will happen a long time from now.

Would this solve the Grounding Problem? Would the metaphysics somehow make it seem plausible that future pain is in itself more significant than past pain? Well, unless our peacemaker adopts the "shrinking block" view (according to which the future exists but the past does not), the metaphysics will not *explain* why future pains matter more than past pains. But maybe no explanation is needed. If the peacemaker has a strong (though perhaps defeasible) conviction that future pain is intrinsically worse than past pain, the metaphysics does nothing to undermine that conviction.

3 Egocentrism and Egocentric Metaphysics

We can make peace between considerations of the greater good and time-biased considerations by adopting an appropriate metaphysical picture. Can we perform an analogous trick for egocentric considerations? What sort of picture would allow us to say that, whenever we favor scenarios in which we are better off, we favor simply better maximal states of affairs? Well, at a minimum the picture would have to imply that, in the "after the train crash" case, where I have a preference that I not suffer, the two possibilities that seem open to me represent different maximal states of affairs, different fully specified ways for everything to be. But since these possibilities differ only with respect to which of the injured parties is *me*, the picture would have to imply that there is a property, *being me*, that somehow enters into states of affairs.

The analogy to four-dimensionalism and its denial should be clear. One way, you might think, for a thing to be is for it to be me. What is this property? What is it for a thing to be this way?

It is natural to think that, if there are any properties in the vicinity of "being me" and "being other," they are relational properties. For example:

(R1)   Being me-relative to CJH.

(R2)   Being other-relative to CJH.

(R3)   Being me-relative to Stalin.

There are many such properties (at least two for every person) and everybody is, in the relevant sense, *on a par* with respect to them—we are all me-relative to ourselves, in virtue of standing in the relation of identity to ourselves, and other-relative to everything else, in virtue of standing in the relation of non-identity to everything else.

But one might take the view, in an effort to advance the peacemaker's project, that there are further, monadic properties:

(M1)   Being me.

(M2)   Being other.

In any given maximal state of affairs, one and only one thing has the monadic property of being me. There is a unique *I* at the center (so to speak) of all that exists. After the train crash, I am comparing maximal states of affairs in which the thing with the monadic property of being me is in pain, with maximal states of affairs in which the thing with the monadic property of being me is free of pain.

Will this not turn out to be just another theory of the kind we considered in chapter one, another theory according to which CJH is metaphysically unique? Well, yes, but if it is to solve the Generalization Problem, then it will need to be considerably more subtle than those were. Let us suppose that I know myself to be CJH, and Jane knows herself to be Jane. And let us suppose that Jane and I are both aware that CJH is to be miserable and Jane content. Our theory will need to explain why, although the state of affairs I am glumly considering is one in which the thing with the monadic property of being me will be miserable, the state of affairs Jane is contentedly considering is one in which the thing with the monadic property of being me will be content. And it will need to explain why I am right to think that the thing with the monadic property of being me will be miserable, and yet Jane is right to think that the thing with monadic property of being me will be content. Why isn't Jane making a mistake?

It may be helpful to see how someone who believes in monadic tensed properties deals with the analogous problem. Let us suppose that it is presently noon, and Joe-at-noon and Joe-at-11:00 a.m. are both aware that Joe-at-noon prospers, and Joe-at-11:00 suffers. Given that he takes *being now* to be a monadic property, the monadic tenser must explain why, although the state of affairs that Joe-at-11:00 glumly considers is one in which Joe's suffering has the monadic property of being now, the state of affairs that Joe-at-noon contentedly considers is one in which Joe's prospering has the monadic property of being now. And he must explain why Joe-at-11:00 is right to think that Joe's suffering has the monadic property of being now, and yet Joe-at-noon is right to think that Joe's prospering has the monadic property of being now. Why isn't Joe-at-11:00 making a mistake?

Obviously this poses no real difficulties for the monadic tenser. Joe-at-11:00 attributed the monadic property of being now to Joe's suffering, and he was right to do so because it was the case, back then, that Joe's suffering had that property. If you are interested in the correctness of Joe-at-11:00's beliefs, the appropriate thing to ask is not "*Is* everything just the way he thought it to be?" but rather "*Was* everything just the way he thought it to be?"

The theory we are groping toward will need a similar trick. In just the way that a monadic tenser has it that the standard by which to judge the correctness of beliefs held at other times is not how things are, but how things were (or will be), so this theory will need to say that the standard by which to judge the correctness of beliefs held by other people is not how things are, but . . . something else.

There are various ways of pulling off the trick. I will outline one, *egocentric presentism*, which seems to me attractive and simple.

3.1 Egocentric Presentism—an Introduction

The best way to introduce this theory is with a story. Imagine that, in a fit of Cartesian pique, I throw away all of my cherished beliefs about how the world is and how I fit into it. I no longer accept that the earth is round, that there are material objects, that I am CJH, or, for that matter, that I am anything at all. In this epistemically emaciated state, I retire to a secluded room and attempt to build up a worldview from the raw materials of what is unquestionably *given*. A series of insights strike me:

Insight 1: There are some things. Seemingly: a painting of Saint George and the Dragon, a telephone, a diary, a facial itch. Their nature remains obscure. Perhaps the painting is not really a painting. Perhaps the telephone is really a toy. Perhaps the diary is really a bundle of sense data. Perhaps the itch is really a neural event. All that can be said for sure is that these things, whatever they are, reveal themselves at this, first stage of the Cartesian exercise. They are *present*.[1]

Insight 2: There is a sentient being, CJH, with all and only the present things as perceptual objects. CJH sees the telephone, painting, and diary. CJH feels the itch.

Insight 3: There are many, many sentient beings other than CJH, but they do not have all and only the present

21

things as perceptual objects. So as to talk about this interesting feature of CJH in an economical way, let us introduce some terms. When someone has all and only present things as perceptual objects, say that he or she has "present experiences." Let "I" (in the nominative, "me" in the accusative) be shorthand for the description "the one with present experiences."

Insight 4: Although I, CJH, am unique in having present experiences, I find that I can imagine other sentient creatures being unique in this respect. I can imagine, for example, that I am Michael Schumacher (that the one with present experiences is Michael Schumacher). This involves imagining that Michael Schumacher's perceptual objects—heat, a smell of foam and latex, the wail of a ten-cylinder engine—are present. It involves imagining hoardings buzzing past me, the one with present experiences, Michael Schumacher, at two hundred miles per hour.

Insight 5: Such imaginings lead me to suspect that I am less unique than I may have thought. Michael Schumacher's experiences are not present, so things are not as I imagined them to be, when I imagined being him. But he has a point of view, and from his point of view things *are* as I imagined them to be—the heat, the foamy smell, and the wail of the engine *are* present. From Michael Schumacher's point of view, Michael Schumacher's experiences are present.

But let us be careful here. In saying that Michael Schumacher has a point of view, I am not taking presence to be a relational property—saying that his perceptual objects are present-relative-to his-point-of-view, whereas mine are present relative-to-my-point-of-view. Presence is a monadic property that my perceptual objects have and his do not.

So what am I saying? Well, it will be helpful to think of the construction "from Michael Schumacher's point of view" as a *one-place intensional operator*. A one-place operator is a lexical item with the following feature: When you attach it to a sentence that expresses a proposition, you get a new sentence that expresses a proposition. Extensional operators are such that the truth value of the new sentence depends only on the truth value of the old sentence. So, for example, "It is not the case that" is an extensional operator. If I attach it to a sentence that expresses a proposition like "it is snowing," I get a new sentence, "It is not the case that it is snowing," that expresses a (new) proposition. And the new sentence is true if and only if the old one is not true. Intensional operators, meanwhile, are such that the truth value of the new sentence does not depend only on the truth value of the old sentence. So, for example, "It is necessarily the case that" is an intensional operator. If I attach it to a sentence that expresses a proposition, "p," then I get a new sentence, "It is necessarily the case that p," that also expresses a proposition. But the truth or falsity of the new sentence depends on more than the truth or falsity of the old one. Learning that "p" is true will not, on its own, tell me whether "It is necessarily the case that p" is true.

When I say "Michael Schumacher's perceptual objects are present," I say that Michael Schumacher's perceptual objects have a monadic property: *being present*. This is not so. But when I add the one-place intensional operator "From Michael Schumacher's point of view" to the sentence, I say something else. What? Just that from Michael Schumacher's point of view, Michael Schumacher's perceptual objects have a monadic property: *being present*.

The notion of a point of view is primitive, so I cannot offer you an informative, reductive account of what it is for it to be the case that from Michael Schumacher's point of view things are a particular way. But I can offer you a helpful way of thinking about points of view. Here it is.

3.2 Semantics for a Logic of Points of View

Say that a *subject world* (henceforth an **S**-world) is a world in which some things are present, and all of those things are perceptual objects of one creature. For shorthand say that that creature has *present experiences*.

At any such world, a set of *atomic* propositions hold true. Think of these as propositions having to do with the way things are, physically speaking, and propositions having to do with where the property of being present is instantiated. So, for example, at $S_{HenryKissinger}$, a world physically identical to our own, but in which the experiences of Henry Kissinger are present, the following atomic propositions hold true:

"The sun orbits the moon"

"There are over ten billion perceiving creatures"

"The person with present experiences was formerly secretary of state"

"CJH's experiences are absent"

Now, let a *system* of **S**-worlds be a set of physically identical **S**-worlds such that for any perceiving creature in an **S**-world in the set, there is an **S**-world in the set in which that very creature has present experiences. And say that for any system of **S**-worlds there is a reflexive two-place access relation, the **a**-relation, defined over pairs of **S**-worlds in the system.

Here, for the sake of having an example to work with, is one system of **S**-worlds:

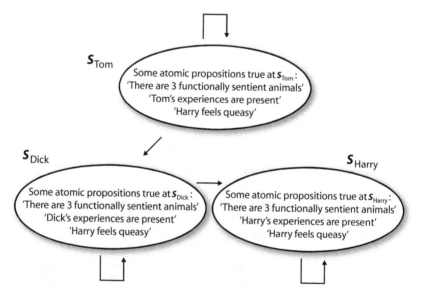

(The ovals represent **S**-worlds. The arrows represent access relations between **S**-worlds: $S_i \rightarrow S_j$ means S_i is **a**-related to S_j.) So, in this system there are three **S**-worlds, S_{Tom}, S_{Dick}, and S_{Harry}. They are all **a**-related to themselves, S_{Tom} is **a**-related to S_{Dick} (though not vice versa), and S_{Dick} is **a**-related to S_{Harry} (though not vice versa).

Now we give truth conditions for propositions containing quantified *point of view* operators in the following way:

Definition 1: From some point of view

⌜*From some point of view* (p)⌝ is true at S_K

$\quad\quad\quad\quad$ iff

for some S_J **a**-related to S_K, p is true at S_J

Definition 2: From every point of view

⌜*From every point of view* (p)⌝ is true at S_K

$\quad\quad\quad\quad$ iff

for every S_J **a**-related to S_K, p is true at S_J

So, for example, in the system shown in the last diagram, the proposition "*From some point of view* (there are present queasy experiences)" is true at S_{Dick}, because S_{Dick} is **a**-related to S_{Harry} and "there are present queasy experiences" is true at S_{Harry}. But it is false at S_{Tom}, because S_{Tom} is not **a**-related to S_{Harry}, or to any other **S**-world at which "there are present queasy experiences" is true.

And we give truth conditions for propositions containing operators of the form "*From Q's point of view*" with the following definition schema:

Definition 3: From the point of view of H

For any functionally sentient being H, $\ulcorner$*from the point of view of H* (p)$\urcorner$ is true at S_K

iff

for some S_J a-related to S_K, $\ulcorner$H has present experiences, and P$\urcorner$ is true at S_J

So in the above system "*from Harry's point of view* (Harry's experiences are present and Harry is queasy)" is true at S_{Dick}. But it is false at S_{Tom}.

Here is a different system, of a kind that will be relevant later:

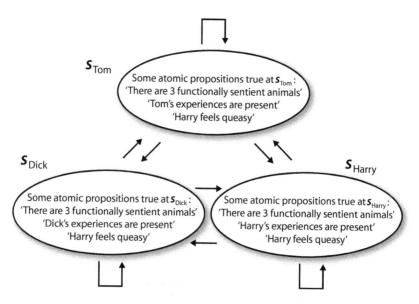

In this system all pairs of **S**-worlds are a-related. So in this system *from Harry's point of view* (Harry has present experiences) is true at every **S**-world. Call this a *maximally interrelated* system.

3.3 Egocentric Presentism and Points of View

That is the **S**-world semantics for propositions like "*from some point of view* (p)." I hope it gives you some intuitive sense of how operators *from some point of view, from every point of view,* etc. (call them *perspectival operators*) work. As an egocentric presentist I believe the semantics to be incorrect but helpful.

I believe it to be incorrect because it says incorrect things about the conditions under which propositions are true or false. Take, for example:

K   "*From Henry Kissinger's point of view* (Henry Kissinger's experiences are present)"

I believe proposition K to be true. But I do not believe that there exists a network of **a**-related **S**-worlds, and the one that I inhabit is **a**-related to some other one in which Henry Kissinger's experiences are present. I believe that all that exists is an **S**-world, S_{ME}, in which the experiences of one person, the person I call "me," are present. That's it. What, then, makes it the case that from Henry's point of view Henry's experiences are present? Nothing more or the less than the fact that from his point of view his experiences are present.

But I believe the **S**-world semantics to be helpful, because propositions containing the *point of view* operators are true or false of this world *as if* it were part of a system of physically identical **S**-worlds and truth conditions for such propositions were given by the **S**-world semantics. (Indeed, supposing I am not a mental solipsist, supposing I believe that everybody has a point of view, and from everybody's point of view everybody has a point of view, and so forth, I will believe that propositions containing the *point of view* operators are true or false of this world as if it were part of a maximally interrelated system of physically identical **S**-worlds, and truth conditions for such propositions were given by the **S**-world semantics.) So the following is helpful advice: Generally, if you want to find out whether a proposition containing some point of view operators is true or false, then assume that our world is part of an appropriate system of physically identical **S**-worlds, apply the definitions given by **S**-world semantics, and you will get the right result. Picturing the system will help you work out the truth values of complicated propositions containing nested perspectival operators like this:

K2 "*From Henry Kissinger's point of view (from Condoleeza Rice's point of view* (Henry Kissinger's experiences are not present))"

It will also help you see how different hypotheses about other people's points of view affect the truth value of propositions containing perspectival operators. For example, to get a grip on the idea that Barack Obama alone lacks a point of view, imagine that this world is a-related to all other **S**-worlds in the system, except for the one in which Barack Obama's experiences are present, and see what follows (it follows, for example, that "*from Barack Obama's point of view* (snow is white)" is false.)

An egocentric presentist's attitude toward the **S**-world semantics, then, is very like a temporal presentist's attitude toward a four-dimensionalist semantics for propositions containing tensed intensional operators, operators like *it was once the case that* and *it will always be the case that*. A four-dimensionalist may offer a semantics like this:

Say that a *moment* is an entity at which a collection of atomic tenseless propositions hold true. For example:

"a football, deformed into the shape of a strawberry, hangs three feet above the turf of Wembley stadium"

"John's mouth lolls open"

Say that a *history* is a set of moments, ordered by an access relation, the *before relation*. And say that within a history, propositions containing tensed operators are true or false at moments, in accordance with the following definitions (I will refer to a moment as an **M**-world.)

Definition 4: It was once the case that

⌜*It was once the case that* (p)⌝ is true at M_K

iff

for some M_J before-related to M_K, p is true at M_J

Definition 5: It has always been the case that

> ⌜*It has always been the case that* (p)⌝ is true at M_K
>
>   iff
>
> for every M_J before-related to M_K, p is true at M_J

and so on and so forth for other tensed operators (like *it will once be the case that*).

A temporal presentist will think of this semantics as incorrect but helpful. It is incorrect because it says incorrect things about the conditions under which propositions are true or false. Take, for example:

B   "*It was once the case that* (Pluto is closer to the Sun than Neptune is)"

This proposition is true, but not in virtue of the fact that there exists a collection of moments, ordered by a before relation, and one in which "Pluto is closer to the Sun than Neptune is" is true is before-related to this moment. There are no past and future moments. All that exists exists now. What, then, makes it the case that B is true? Nothing more or less than the fact that Pluto was once closer to the Sun than Neptune was.

But the four-dimensionalist semantics is helpful, because propositions containing tensed operators are true or false of this moment, the moment, as if it were part of a succession of moments, ordered by a before relation, and truth conditions for such propositions were given by the four-dimensionalist semantics. So the following is good advice: Generally, if you want to find out if a proposition containing tensed operators is true or false, then imagine that this moment is one of a succession of moments, appropriately ordered by a before relation, apply the definitions given by the four-dimensionalist semantics, and you will get the right result. Doing this will help you work out the truth value of complicated propositions, containing many nested operators, like this:

B2   "*It was once the case that* (*it was always the case that* (*it will once be the case that* (Pluto is closer to the sun than Neptune is)))"

It will also help you to get a grip on how different hypotheses about the nature of time affect the truth value of tensed propositions. For example, to get a grip on the idea that time is non-branching, you can imagine moments ordered by a nonbranching before-relation and see what follows. To get a grip on the idea of discontinuous time, you can imagine a pair of moments with no intervening one and see what follows. To get a grip on the idea of cyclical time, imagine a cyclical before-relation and see what follows.

The attitude is also very like a modal fictionalist's attitude to the possible worlds semantics for modal logic.[2] The modal fictionalist believes that propositions containing modal operators (like *it is possible that* and *it is necessary that*) are true or false of the actual world *as if* it were part of a wider system of possible worlds ordered by an access relation, and truth conditions for the operators were given by the possible worlds semantics. So, says the fictionalist, when you are thinking about what is necessary, what is possible, what might have happened if you had done something, and so forth, go ahead and suppose the wider system exists. That will bring precision and rigor to your modal thinking. But do not be fooled into believing that the wider system really does exist. Only the actual world exists.

3.4 Egocentric Presentism and Egocentric Considerations

If egocentric presentism is right, then an **S**-world is all there is. So an egocentic presentist can make peace between the considerations that move a mild egocentric hedonist and considerations of the greater good by taking **S**-worlds in which I (shorthand for "the one with present experiences," remember) suffer to be worse simpliciter than other-things-equal **S**-worlds in which I do not. This will enable her to believe

(Harmony) Whenever a mild egocentric hedonist favors a situation in which she suffers less, she thereby favors a simply better maximal state of affairs.

while avoiding the three obstacles that appeared to stand in her way. Let me explain why.

The Problem of Irreducibly Egocentric Preferences

In the "after the train crash" case, recall, mild egocentric hedonism dictates that I favor a scenario in which I do not suffer, namely:

Scenario (1):

CJH suffers	Joe Bloggs is comfortable
	↑ And this is *me*

over a scenario in which I do, namely:

Scenario (2):

CJH suffers	Joe Bloggs is comfortable
↑ And this is *me*	

The problem was that scenarios (1) and (2) do not appear to represent different fully specified ways for everything to be, different maximal states of affairs. So cases like this appear to be counterexamples to (Harmony). But if egocentric presentism is correct, then scenarios (1) and (2) do represent different maximal states of affairs. The first represents one in which there is present comfort, the second represents one in which there is present suffering. And, given that all other things are appropriately equal, this makes the first better simpliciter than the second.

The Generalization Problem

In the "competing for a scarce resource" case, recall, mild hedonistic egoism dictates that I (knowing myself to be CJH) favor my getting the scarce resource, and Jane (knowing herself to be Jane) favor her getting the scarce resource. But the problem was that there appear to be only two ways everything might be:

Way (1)

CJH gets the resource and is content	Jane misses out and is miserable

Way (2)

CJH misses out and is miserable	Jane gets the resource and is content

Jane seems to be favoring Way (2) over (1). I seem to be favoring Way (1) over Way (2). But it cannot both be better that the maximal state of affairs represented by Way (1) obtains, and that the maximal state of affairs represented by Way (2) does. So this seems like another counterexample to (Harmony).

But if egocentric presentism is correct, there are really four ways everything might be:

Way (1)	CJH gets the resource and there is present contentedness	Jane misses out and there is absent misery
Way (2)	CJH misses out and there is present misery	Jane gets the resource and there is absent contentedness
Way (3)	CJH gets the resource and there is absent contentedness	Jane misses out and there is present misery
Way (4)	CJH misses out and there is absent misery	Jane gets the resource and there is present contentedness

In favoring my getting the resource, I am favoring (1) over (2), and so I should, for (1) is the better state of affairs. But how should I think about what Jane is doing when she favors her getting the resource?

There are really two questions here (for recall that one way to favor a state of affairs is to bring it about, another is to desire that it come about). First, suppose that Jane gets herself the resource. Has she brought about a better state of affairs? Second, suppose that she desires that she get the resource. Is she desiring that a better state of affairs obtain?

The answer to the first question may seem straightforward. When Jane gets herself the resource, she brings about state of affairs (2), in which there is present misery. If she had brought it about that CJH got the resource, then she would have brought about state of affairs (1), in which there is present contentedness. From this it may seem natural to conclude that, although egocentric hedonistic considerations counted in favor of her getting the resource for herself, considerations of the greater good did not. She brought about a worse state of affairs.

Thought about this way, the pleasing harmony between egocentric hedonistic considerations and considerations of the greater good is granted to CJH and CJH alone. For everybody else, considerations of the greater good count in favor of their making the world more pleasant and comfortable for him.

But there is another, much better way to think about how considerations of the greater good bear on Jane's decision. When I treat another person as a practical deliberator and ask whether such and such considerations support her doing so-and-so, I imagine being in her position, in a particular deliberative context, facing choices, options, and alternatives. This involves taking the deliberative context to be *present*. It involves taking the world to be just as, from her point of view, it is.

Thought about this way, the true observation that is relevant to assessing whether or not Jane's decision to get the resource for herself was supported by considerations of the greater good is not:

By getting herself the resource, Jane brought about state of affairs (2) rather than state of affairs (1). But (1) is better than (2).

but rather:

From Jane's point of view (by getting herself the resource she brought about state of affairs (4) rather than state of affairs (3)). And (3) is better than (4).

And the general formula for determining whether considerations of the greater good support another person, A, doing something is not:

The Wrong Way to Think About Considerations of the Greater Good

When A has options $O_1, \ldots, O_n$, considerations of the greater good support her taking O_i

iff

S_i is the best of $S_1, \ldots, S_n$ where $S_1, \ldots, S_n$ are the states of affairs such that S_1 will come about if A takes $O_1, \ldots$, and S_n will come about if A takes O_n.

but rather:

The Right Way to Think About Considerations of the Greater Good

> When A has options $O_1, \ldots, O_n$, considerations of the greater good support her taking O_i
>
> $$iff$$
>
> S_i is the best of $S_1, \ldots, S_n$—where $S_1, \ldots, S_n$ are the states of affairs such that *From A's point of view* (S_1 will come about if A takes $O_1, \ldots,$ and S_n will come about if A takes O_n).

To see what an arbitrary other person ought, vis-à-vis promoting the greater good, to do, we consider the states affairs that, from her point of view, she is in a position to bring about, and ask which is best.

So much for Jane's bringing it about that she suffers less. Let us turn to the second question. What if she just desires that she suffers less? Is she, then, desiring that the greater good come about? To answer this question we must take a view about what it is she desires or believes when she has a desire or belief that she might express like this: ". . . that I, Jane, will comfortable, and he, CJH, will be the one who suffers." The natural thing to say is that she desires or believes that things will be Way (4). As well she should, because (4) is a good way for things to be.

Now suppose that, as a matter of fact, Jane will get the resource. As a matter of fact, the one with present experiences (CJH) will suffer. So is her desire satisfied? Is her belief correct? Yes and yes. Just as someone who believes in monadic tensed properties takes it that, when dealing with past desires and beliefs, the measure of whether they are satisfied or correct is not how things are, but how things were, so the egocentric presentist takes it that, when dealing with another person's desires and beliefs, the measure of whether they are satisfied or correct is not how things are, but how, from her point view, things are. In this case *from Jane's point of view* (the one with present experiences does not suffer), so Jane's desire that she not suffer is satisfied, and Jane's belief that she will not suffer is correct.

The Grounding Problem

Last, what about the Grounding Problem? Would the metaphysics support mild egocentric hedonism by providing grounds for thinking that, all other things being equal, it is worse that suffering be mine than someone else's? I think so. If you do not see this immediately, I urge you (really!) to perform this experiment:

Trial by Kettle | Today, many hundreds of Russians will spill boiling water on their hands. Pour boiling water on your own hand and compare your present discomfort with the absent discomfort of the northern-most Russian spiller. Which is worse?

Your immediate reaction, "This pain is dreadful, worse than any of those Russian pains" may be tempered by a sober, reflective thought:

"My pain appears worse to me because I am more intimately acquainted with it. It is present to me in a way that the northern-most Russian spiller's pain is not. But he is more intimately acquainted with his pain. It is present to him in a way that mine is not. Since our situations are really symmetrical, I find, on reflection, that I have no grounds for thinking that my pain is worse simpliciter than his pain."

Well and good, but this humbling thought is not available to an egocentric presentist. For an egocentric presentist, the situations are not symmetrical. It is not that my pain is present to me and his present to him. Mine is present and his is absent. That is part of the way things are. So there is no reason to qualify or reassess my initial judgment.

The thought experiment does not, of course, commit an egocentric presentist to extreme egocentric hedonism—the view that only present suffering has any significance at all. It identifies one factor that makes pleasure better and suffering worse. This is quite compatible with thinking that, in evaluating the significance of suffering, there are many other relevant factors to consider, such as the *intensity* of the suffering, the *duration* of the suffering, and the *number* of sufferers. It may be very tricky to give these factors precise weight. Is it better that there be one hour of hand scald-ing or four hours of thumb scalding? Is it better that there be one scalded hand or four scalded thumbs?[3] Is it better that there be absent suffering from hand scalding or present suffering from thumb scalding? But some cases are less tricky. It is better that there be four hangnails than one crushed leg. It is better that there be present suffering from a hangnail than absent suffering from of leg crushing. After all, when there is absent suffering from leg crushing, and the victim is not a zombie, it is the case that *from someone else's point of view* (there is excruciating pain). And an egocentric presentist is free to take it that this matters, in just the way that a monadic tenser is free to take it that it matters that *it will be the case that* (there is excruciating pain). That is why empathy is instructive. For an egocentric presentist, empathiz-ing with an unfortunate involves imagining that the unfortunate has present experiences. This involves viscerally imagining what *from the unfortunate's point of view* (is the case). And egocentric presentists may care about the results of this exercise because they care about what *from another person's point of view* (is the case).

So if I, a mild egocentric hedonist, adopt egocentric presentism, in some cases (e.g., comparing a state of affairs in which I suffer a hangnail with one in which someone else suffers a crushed leg) I will still face a conflict between egocentric-hedonistic consid-erations and considerations of the greater good. But the residual conflict will not trouble me. As an egocentric presentist, I do not take egocentric-hedonistic considerations to be considerations of a special, distinctive kind, that count toward my favoring one state of affairs over another even when I recognize that the other is bet-ter simpliciter than the one. Once I have judged that it is better that there be a present hangnail than absent leg crushing, it is not as if there is some further consideration—"but the hangnail will be mine!"—that has independent force. I have already accounted for the presence of the hangnail, the fact that it is mine, in my judgment about which state of affairs is better simpliciter. So when egocentric-hedonistic considerations and considerations of the greater good conflict, the former just fall away.

Furthermore, when the trade-off between my interests and the interests of other people is more evenly balanced, as an egocentric presentist I can indulge my mildly egocentric preferences and attend to my own pleasures and pains while enjoying the psychological harmony of Louis XIV—the serene confidence that comes with believing that in doing what is good for me I am doing what is good full stop.

3.5 Can We Resolve All Conflicts This Way?

Let us take stock of where we are. As a mild egocentric hedonist embedded in a community of mild egocentric hedonists, I cannot help but notice that there is a systemic conflict between my aims and the aims of other people. Facing this conflict, I perform a trick. The trick enables me both to think that my disproportionate concern for my own suffering is vindicated by considerations of the greater good, and to think that the disproportionate concern of other people for their own suffering is vindicated by considerations of the greater good. I am not making any kind of mistake, and neither are they.

But widespread mild egocentric hedonism is not the only source of systemic conflict between my aims and the aims of other people. Such conflicts arise whenever other people have tastes, priorities, or values different from mine. Can I, and should I, generalize the trick?

Well, sometimes the trick will not be helpful. Sometimes, faced with people whose aims are at odds with mine, I feel very little pressure to think that those people are not making any kind of mistake. For example: I am sharing a car with an avid fan of 1980s pop icon Rick Astley. I want the music to stop, she wants it to continue. But she is *wrong*. Astley's songs are terrible. For another example: The FA Cup Final has gone to penalties. Ronaldo steps up. I want his penalty to float like a soap bubble over the bar and out of the stadium. A million Manchester United fans want otherwise. But they are *wrong*. Manchester United represents all that is ugly and boorish and brazenly commercial in football.

The trick will be helpful only in cases where I think it is right and fitting that other people's aims conflict with mine, when I accept what moral philosophers call an *agent-relative deontic theory*.[4] Certainly there are many cases, egocentric hedonism aside, in which I do this. For example, I tend to favor, all other things being equal, the prospering of people with whom I am intimate over the prospering of strangers (although this tendency is riddled with exceptions—I am not so very pious and holy as to be bemused by Gore Vidal's remark, "When a friend succeeds, a little something in me dies"). And I expect others to do the same. Indeed, I think that others ought to do the same. Does egocentric presentism allow me to think that my disproportionate concern for people with whom I am intimate is vindicated by the greater good, and that others are not making any kind of mistake in being disproportionately concerned with the people with whom they are intimate?

It does not. To see why, let us consider a particular example of disproportionate concern, not so far away from mild egocentric hedonism: I have a five-year-old daughter, TGH. I care a lot about her comfort. If much pain is going to fall on the heads of little girls tomorrow, I would rather that none of it fall on her. And I think it right and fitting that I have this attitude. And I think it right and fitting that other fathers take a similar attitude toward their daughters.

In this case, the idea would be to stipulate that suffering endured by the daughter of the one all of whose perceptual objects are present is worse than suffering endured by the daughter of someone some of whose perceptual objects are absent. But it is not going to work, because, even if I could somehow persuade myself to accept the evaluative claim (And why would I do this? Why would I believe that absent suffering that bears this one indirect relation to presence is worse than absent suffering that bears some other indirect relation to presence?), this would not dignify the kind of disproportionate concern I have for my daughter.

What exactly is it, the disproportionate concern I have for my daughter? I could loosely describe it like this: "I want my daughter to be comfortable." But there is ambiguity in that description. I might be saying that I want my daughter, *whoever she happens to be*, to be comfortable—among situations in which I have one daughter, all and only ones in which I have one comfortable daughter satisfy my desire. Or I might be taking it that I have a daughter, TGH, and saying that I want *TGH* to be comfortable—all and only situations in which TGH is comfortable satisfy my desire. There is a difference between these two sorts of desire, a difference that will show up when I come to doubt whether TGH is my daughter.

There is just the same ambiguity in: "I want myself to be comfortable." I might be saying that I want myself, whoever I turn out to be, to be comfortable—all and only situations in which I am comfortable satisfy my desire. Or I might be taking it that I am a fellow, CJH, and saying that I want CJH to be comfortable— all and only situations in which CJH is comfortable satisfy my desire.

The desire that underlies my disproportionate concern for my own comfort is clearly of the first kind. It is a desire, first and foremost, that *I* not suffer. I am a fickle friend of CJH. I care about his comfort for only as long as I take him to be me. The "after the train crash" case illustrates this. When I become confused about who I am, my immediate thought is, "I don't care about whether CJH or Joe Bloggs is to be operated on, just so long as it isn't *me!*"

But no analogous desire underlies my disproportionate concern for my daughter's comfort. Consider this case:

> *After a Second Train Crash* | I wake up in the hospital once again, once again swathed in plaster. The television on the wall tells me that CJH and Joe Bloggs have been pulled from the wreckage of a second crash, but this time their cumulative injuries are so severe that neither will survive the day. "Oops!" I think. "Whoever I am, I am a goner." But the television offers me some consolation. CJH has a daughter, TGH. Joe Bloggs has a daughter, Jane Bloggs. TGH is like so ... Jane Bloggs is like so ..."Interesting" I think, "I now know a tremendous amount about TGH and Jane Bloggs, though I don't know which is my daughter." Finally the television tells me that one of the girls is scheduled to have an extremely long and painful operation in a few hours time.

I speculate that I would not, in this situation, be struck by the thought, "I don't care about whether TGH or Jane Bloggs is to be operated on, just so long as it isn't *my* daughter!" And there is a reason why. What makes her suffering so awful, in my eyes, is not the fact that it is my daughter's, but the fact that it is TGH's.[5] The desire that underlies my disproportionate concern for her is of the second kind. But egocentric presentism, combined with an appropriate axiology, can only dignify desires of the first kind.

What other desires of the first kind do we have? I suspect rather few. Even when it comes to desires on my own behalf, there are many things I want for myself other than comfort, but I think that I want most of those things in the first way. I think that I want CJH to be wise, beloved, and good, but I do not particularly want myself to be wise, beloved, and good.

So egocentric presentism is a very specialized tool, designed to make sense of a kind of desire that is (at least in me) rather unusual.

4 Clarifications

By adopting egocentric presentism you can harmonize your otherwise discordant impulses to make the world better and to make the world a more pleasant place for you to live in. Well and good. But you can often rid yourself of psychological conflict by adopting a suitably contrived worldview. If you believe in a paradisiacal afterlife, then you will go peaceably to your death. If you believe that meat is a kind of root vegetable, then you will not feel too bad about eating it. Unless egocentric presentism is an independently plausible theory, the moral of the previous chapters is strictly academic.

Is egocentric presentism an independently plausible theory? I think so, though it is very easily misunderstood. In this chapter I will try to clarify the theory, in an effort to head off such misunderstandings. In the next I will point to some further benefits that come with adopting it.

4.1 Ontological Commitments

I said that an egocentric presentist believes that only one subject world exists. There are no other subject worlds. You may be tempted to think, then, that the view is a view about *ontology* in a narrow sense of the term, a view about what things exist. And, given that there is a solipsistic flavor to the view, you may be tempted to think of it as a kind of ontological solipsism, a view according to which other people have diminished ontological status. Believing egocentric presentism is kind of like believing:

There are no other people

Other people are spectral entities, like angels

Other people are abstract objects, like numbers and sets

Other people are figments of my imagination

Other people exist only while I exist

But this is not right. Other subject worlds aside, egocentric presentism is quite neutral about what sorts of things there are. To say that the world is a subject world is just to say that, of the things there are, some of them are monadically present, and there is a sentient creature with all and only those things as perceptual objects. This in no way threatens the (natural enough) idea that many people exist, and they are all equally real, fleshy and (to mix metaphors), concrete. People are not any more or less real, fleshy, or concrete for having or failing to have monadically present perceptual objects.

In brief, you do not get to be an egocentric presentist by removing things from your picture of the world. You get to be one by adding some facts to your picture of the world: facts about which things are present and facts about how, from points of view, things are.

4.2 Presence and Consciousness

Egocentric presentists deny that other people have present experiences. You may be tempted to think they are thereby denying that other people are conscious. You may be tempted to think them mental solipsists.

Again, this is not right. Egocentric presentists will certainly not think that, to be conscious, it is necessary that you have present experiences, although how, precisely, they construe the relation between presence and consciousness will depend heavily on their views about consciousness. Some philosophers think that consciousness supervenes on the physical. To be conscious it suffices, roughly, to be in possession of a brain that is organized in a certain way, interacting with an environment in a certain way—where the "certain way"s can, at least in principle, be specified in the language of the natural sciences. Facts about presence and absence will, on this view, have nothing at all to do with facts about consciousness. Others think that consciousness is a more elusive and mysterious thing. These philosophers can use egocentric presentism to pin down the elusive and mysterious thing they are talking about.

Here is a natural way of thinking about what I do when I take, for example, Barack Obama to be conscious in the elusive and mysterious sense. I imagine being him. I imagine looking out of the window of my office, at a birch tree, its branches stretched into threads by the thick, bulletproof glass. Then I take it that the world has a feature in virtue of which I have gotten my imagining right or wrong. There is something it is like to be Barack Obama. If it is just like I imagined it, then I got it right. If it is not just like I imagined it, if it is somehow different, then I got it wrong.

For the egocentric presentist, imagining being Barack Obama, looking out of the window, involves imagining that Barack Obama's experiences are present. And there is a natural candidate for the feature of the world in virtue of which I have gotten my imagining right or wrong: the way that, from Barack Obama's point of view, things are. If I imagine things to be just the way that, from Barack Obama's point of view, things are, then I got my imagining right.

So what makes it the case that there is something it is like to be Barack Obama, on this way of thinking, is the fact that *from Barack Obama's point of view* (Barack Obama's experiences are present). Generally:

Consciousness

> A is conscious iff *from A's point of view* (A's experiences are present)

Call a person who meets the physicalist's standards for consciousness, but who is not conscious in this more exotic sense of the term, a *zombie*. Level-headed egocentric presentists will take it that other people possess points of view, and that from their points of view their experiences are present. There are no zombies. But no feature of the formal structure of egocentric presentism commits them to thinking this. As an egocentric presentist I have the conceptual resources to describe a world in which Barack Obama alone is a zombie. Here is one way of representing the facts about points of view in such a world, S_{ME1} (I have placed the bottom half of the diagram in a gray box to remind you that S_{ME1} is all that exists, but propositions containing the point of view operators are true or false, as if it were part of the network below it in figure 4.1 and truth conditions for such propositions were given by the S-world semantics):

Figure 4.1: Barack Obama Is a Zombie

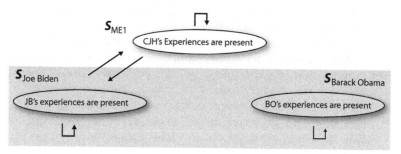

CJH's experiences are present, *from Joe Biden's point of view* (Joe Biden's experiences are present), *from Joe Biden's point of view* (*from CJH's point of view* (CJH's experiences are present)), etc. But it is not the case that *from Barack Obama's point of view* (Barack Obama's experiences are present).

I also have the conceptual resources to describe a world in which CJH is a zombie. Here is a way of representing facts about one such world, S_{ME2}, a world in which I am Barack Obama:

Figure 4.2: CJH Is a Zombie

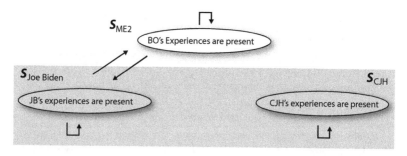

Barack Obama's experiences are present, *from Joe Biden's point of view* (Joe Biden experiences are present), etc. But it is not the case that *from CJH's point of view* (CJH's experiences are present).

I even have conceptual resources to describe a world in which everybody is a zombie. There are two ways to do this. One is to suppose that it is not the case that *from someone's point of view* (someone has present experiences), while supposing that someone has present experiences. Facts about presence and points of view are as in S_{ME3}:

Figure 4.3: Zombie World

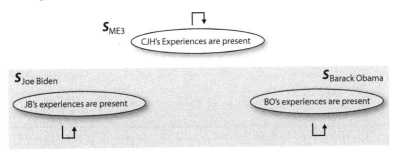

The other way to get a zombie world is to suppose, again, that it is not the case that *from someone's point of view* (someone has present experiences), and suppose that nobody's experiences are present. We cannot represent this with a system of **S**-worlds, because it involves denying the central thesis of egocentric presentism (the thesis that one and only one person has present experiences). But I see no reason for the egocentric presentist to deem it metaphysically impossible. An egocentric presentist thinks it contingent, of any given person, that they have present experiences. So why not think it contingent that someone has present experiences? As an egocentric presentist I readily accept the possibility of a world in which CJH alone has present experiences. So why not accept the possibility of a world just like this one, but in which CJH does not exist?

In brief: Adopting egocentric presentism does not commit you to any particular view about what consciousness is or about who is or is not conscious. It does, however, give you conceptual resources to understand what it might be for someone to be conscious in the exotic sense imagined by nonreductionists about the mental.

4.3 Presence and Time

When I introduced egocentric presentism, I leaned hard on analogies between the metaphysics of the self and the metaphysics of time. You might be tempted to think, then, that an egocentric presentist is committed to taking some view or other about the metaphysics of time.

The most closely analogous theory is the moving-spotlight theory of time, which combines an expansive, block-universe ontology (according to which past, present, and future objects, events, moments exist) with the claim that one moment is privileged (tensed properties are monadic and only one moment thas the monadic property of *being-now*). Egocentric presentism likewise combines a generous ontology (according to which other people exist) with the claim that one person is privileged (such that all and only his or her perceptual objects are present). But it is just an analogy. Egocentric presentism is not the same as any theory of time, because it does not have the same subject matter: Being present is not the same as being-now.

Things that are-now may not be present. Nelson's Column exists now, but it is not present.

Things that are present may not be-now. I look through a telescope, far into the distant reaches of the universe. There, a hundred million light-years away, is a dying star. The star is present,[1] though it long ago ceased to exist.[2]

Indeed, two things may both be present without even existing at the same time. There is the dying star, and there, a thousand light-years away, is a fledgling star. Both stars are present, though one ceased to exist long before the other came into existence.

And perhaps it is just as well that egocentric presentism is not a theory of time, because there are powerful objections against theories of time that dignify a slice of history in one way or another, objections that do not carry over to egocentric presentism.

One charge that has been leveled against temporal presentism (the view that only things that exist-now exist) is that there are intuitively true propositions for which the temporal presentist (armed only with a spare ontology and the operators *it will be the case that, it was the case that, in five minutes it will be the case that,* etc.) cannot give truth conditions.[3] For example, propositions that seem to involve a count of things that exist at different times, like "There have been three kings of England named George" and propositions that seem to invoke relations between things that exist at different times, like: "I am a big fan of Jane Austen" and "Lincoln and I have stood in the very same place."

Maybe this is a serious problem, maybe it is not. But there is no analogous problem for egocentric presentists, no intuitively true proposition for which they cannot give truth conditions. There is a reason for this. The problems arise for those who deny that past and future things exist because their picture is significantly more economical than that of their opponents, but the egocentric presentists's have a picture that is significantly more opulent than that of their opponents. They get egocentric presentism by taking their opponents' picture and *adding* facts (facts about which experiences are monadically present, which monadically absent, and about how, from the points of view of other people, things are). So egocentric presentists have all of the semantic resources that are available to their opponents, and more.

Advocates of the moving-spotlight theory have a similar wealth of resources at their disposal. But the moving-spotlight theory has problems of its own. One worry is that it needs to appeal to an infinity of time dimensions to make sense of the idea that the fact about which moment is now changes as time goes by. "You imagine that the now moves along the time dimension of the four-dimensional block universe like a spotlight," says the objector. "If it moves then it must move at some rate. At what rate? n seconds of time per unit measure of what, hypertime? But if there is hypertime, then surely you think there must be a moment in hypertime that is monadically hypernow and that this changes, that the hypernow *moves* along the hypertime dimension of the five-dimensional block universe (unless you just want to be a five-dimensional block-universe theorist, which seems like a weird resting point). If the hypernow moves, then it must move at some rate. At what rate? n units of hypertime per unit measure of what, hyperhypertime? But if there is hyperhyper-time," etc.

Again, this may or may not be a serious problem for the moving-spotlight theory, but there is no analogous problem for the egocentric presentist.[4] One person's experiences are present; from the point of view of other people, their experiences are present. That is all an egocentric presentist needs to say.

Finally, the problem that many philosophers have considered fatal for the moving-spotlight view, temporal presentism—indeed all views that dignify a slice of history—is their apparent inconsistency with Special Relativity.[5] Right now I am clapping my hands. Call this event c. Take some distant hand-clapping, e. Is e occurring now? Well that depends, presumably, on whether e occurs simultaneously with c. But Special Relativity tells us that there is no such thing as absolute simultaneity. e may occur simultaneously with c relative to some rest frames, prior to c relative to some other rest frames, and after c relative to yet other rest frames. So the best we can say is that e is now-relative to some rest frames, past-relative to others, and future-relative to yet others. But then we seem to have given up on the idea that tensed properties are monadic.

But again, whether or not this is a serious problem for views that dignify a slice of history, there are no analogous problems for egocentric presentism, because no scientifically contentious notions (like the notion of simultaneity) are built into the theory.

My broad point here is that, whereas there may be structural affinities between theories that dignify the self and theories that dignify a slice of history, there are two orthogonal issues at stake. If you think that theories that dignify a slice of history do not survive sustained critical inspection, then you can still be a four-dimensionalist egocentric presentist. Indeed, I find that an attractive position.

I find it attractive because I think that egocentric presentism is a better theory than any theory that dignifies a slice of history, because I think that the big idea that appears to support such theories really supports egocentric presentism. What moves people to reject four-dimensionalism? It is not, I take it, that they see that our best scientific theories build tense into the world in a way that the four-dimensionalist cannot account for. It is rather that they are unable to square four-dimensionalism with the way they experience the world. It is a crucial part of the phenomenology of experience that certain events are distinguished.

I feel the pull of this intuition very strongly. Certain events *are* distinguished: the stuttering patter of fingers against a keyboard, the frenzied efforts of a fly to pass through a pane of glass, the passage of a pendulous rain cloud over the streets of Boston. And once I have felt its pull, it is easy to make what I will call (using entirely nonprejudicial language) the *big mistake.* The big mistake: a misguided sense of humility drives me to conclude that the distinguishing feature of these events (the stuttering patter of the fingers, the efforts of the fly, the passage of the cloud) must be shared by some wider class of events. After all, these events are all happening in the immediate vicinity of CJH; indeed they are all events of which CJH is aware, and there surely cannot be a sphere of distinction surrounding CJH! So I say that these events (the stuttering patter of the fingers, etc.) *and all events that occur at the same time* are distinguished. All events simultaneous with these have a feature (for a temporal presentist: existence, for a moving-spotlight theorist: the property of being-now) that cannot be found elsewhere in world history.

The big mistake is, for several reasons, a big mistake. For one thing, if there is a lack of humility in the thought that, of all the untold trillions of events in known world history, the ones I am aware of, alone, are metaphysically distinguished, there is hardly more humility in the thought that, of all the untold billions of years in known world history, the one I live in, alone, is metaphysically distinguished. For another thing, the extension seems arbitrary: Why say that these events and all events that occur at the same time have the distinguished feature? Why not say, for example, that these events and all events that occur in the same place have the distinguished feature? Furthermore, when I widened the class of distinguished events, I made use of a notion, simultaneity, that falls under the authority of natural science. It is up to natural science to tell us about the nature of simultaneity. If, as appears to be the case, it tells us that there is no such thing as absolute simultaneity, then I will forced to revise my views about the special property I am attributing to events.

Better to take the original intuition at face value. These events (the stuttering patter of the fingers, etc.) and no others are distinguished.

4.4 The Intelligibility of the Notion of Monadic Presence

What is it for a thing to be present? Not present to me or present to you, just present? To understand egocentric presentism, you will need to have a grip on this notion of monadic presence.

In an effort to give you a grip, I asked you to try out some Cartesian introspection: Wipe your epistemic slate clean. Forget where you are, forget who you are, forget that you are anybody at all. Now attend to the world. You will find that there are certain things. Take their appearing at this stage of introspection to be a feature of the things, not a feature of how they appear to you. They are present.

This may seem like a very strenuous mental exercise. You may be tempted to infer that the notion of presence is like plutonium. It is the sort of thing that can be brought into existence only by many hours of painstaking labor inside a philosophical laboratory. Outside of philosophical laboratories it is nowhere to be found.

But again, I think this is not right. I think it is at least possible to have a pre-theoretical grip on the notion of monadic presence. Consider my childhood. When I was a child I was possessed by all kinds of quasi-solipsistic fantasies, convinced that the people around me were all aliens or actors or robots or secret agents or whatever. So far so normal. As I grew up so I grew out of this phase. I stopped jumping around doors to catch the aliens off guard and generally became more mellow. But one quasi-solipsistic thought survived into my adolescence. It would arise most distinctively when I thought about death. What would my death be like? I would imagine a vicious internal cramp as my heart gives out, panic and fear as my muscles become limp and, as the blood stagnates in my head and my brain starves of oxygen, what? My school vicar said light. Homer, in a much more impressive way, said darkness:

Achilles smote him with his sword and killed him. He struck him in the belly near the navel, so that all his bowels came gushing out on to the ground, and the darkness of death came over him as he lay gasping.[6]

The sword reeked with his blood, while dark death and the strong hand of fate gripped him and closed his eyes. Idomeneus speared Erymas in the mouth; the bronze point of the spear went clean through it beneath the brain, crashing in among the white bones and smashing them up. His teeth were all of them knocked out and the blood came gushing in a stream from both his eyes; it also came gurgling up from his mouth and nostrils, and the darkness of death enfolded him round about.[7]

But even then I understood that neither was right. After my death there would be a kind of nothingness, a kind of absence that was difficult to describe or imagine. The closest I could come to picking it out with words was by appeal to precedent—things would be the way they were before I was born.

But now I was struck by a thought. Isn't it amazing and weird that for millions of years, generation after generation of sentient creatures came into being and died, came into being and died, and all the while there was this absence, and then one creature, CJH, unexceptional in all physical and psychological respects, came into being, and POW! Suddenly there were present things!

Was I thinking about presence and absence in a relational sense? Clearly not, for there is nothing at all amazing or weird about the fact that for millions of years sentient creatures existed without things being present to CJH, and then CJH was born and suddenly things were present to CJH. To the extent that I found it amazing and weird that CJH's birth brought an end to millions of years of absence, I must have been thinking about presence and absence in the monadic sense.

So the notion of monadic presence is at least sufficiently intuitive for a thirteen-year-old with no exposure to philosophy to grasp it and find it perplexing (putting aside, for the moment, the question of whether the thirteen-year-old *should* have found it perplexing.)

4.5 Making Sense of What Other People Believe and Say

An egocentric presentist uses "I" as shorthand for "the one with present experiences." You might be tempted to think, then, that he will be unable to make sense of what other egocentric presentists are doing when they use the same term in the same way. Are they referring to him? They certainly do not take themselves to be doing that. But *he* is the one with present experiences, so what is going on?

To fix ideas let us suppose that I, an egocentric presentist, am faced by Mary, another egocentric presentist, and from Mary's mouth come the words: "I am female." It is natural for me to think that there is something that Mary says. Philosophers of language call this, the something she says, the *proposition she expresses*. What is it? And it is natural for me to think that what she says must have a feature: true, false, or neither. Philosophers of language call this the *truth value of the proposition*. What is it? There are at least three different views I could take about this: strict falsehood; context-sensitive expression; or no expression.

Strict Falsehood

I could think that the proposition Mary expresses is

P   That the one with present experiences is female.

And it is false, because the one with present experiences is male. Indeed, most of what other egocentric presentists say is false. When my egocentric presentist daughter whines "I am hungry!" she says something false. I have just had a very good lunch. When a student comes up to me and says, "I just can't stand reading all this philosophy" he says something false. I quite enjoy reading philosophy.

This may seem like a strange view, but please keep two important qualifications in mind. First, for practical purposes this egocentric presentist will usually care very little about whether the self-involving propositions expressed by other people are true or false. When Bejing radio tells me that the greatest leader of the modern era is still alive, I do not care at all about whether the expressed proposition is true. I care about whether a proposition in its vicinity is true. By "the greatest leader of the modern era," the radio announcer intends to refer to Mao. Can Mao really still be alive?[8] When my egocentric presentist mother calls me up and says, "Guess what—I have moved to Havana!" I do not care whether the expressed proposition is true. I care about whether a proposition in its vicinity is true. By "I" my mother means to refer to my mother. Can she really have moved to Havana?

Second, even in the context of theoretical discussions of egocentric presentism, the egocentric presentist will, for different reasons, care very little about whether the self-involving propositions expressed by other people are true or false. As an egocentric presentist, I think that other people are right in believing and asserting that their own experiences are present.[9] So Mary is right to express the false proposition P. And, in the context of a philosophical discussion, I care more about whether my interlocutors are right to say what they say, believe what they believe, than I care about whether what they say and believe is true.

This may sound like a very grand, radical position to take. After all, it involves denying that truth is the measure of correctness of belief and assertion.

It is correct for M to assert that P iff P is true.

It is correct for M to believe that P iff P is true.

But the position is less radical than it appears. Something close to truth is the measure of correctness of belief and assertion.

It is correct for M to assert that P iff *from M's point of view* (P is true).[10]

It is correct for M to believe that P iff *from M's point of view* (P is true).

Context-Sensitive Expression

Alternatively, I could think that the proposition Mary expresses is not

P   That the one with present experiences is female.

but

P*   That *from Mary's point of view* (the one with present experiences is female).

And it is true, because it is indeed the case that from Mary's point of view the one with present experiences is female.

The general idea would be that the nature of the proposition expressed by an utterance may depend on whether the utterer has present or absent experiences. Mary has absent experiences, so she expresses P*. But *from Mary's point of view* (Mary has present experiences) so *from Mary's point of view* (Mary expresses P). And that is all good, because P* is true and *from Mary's point of view* (P is true). So she says something true, and from her point of view she says something true.

There is an advantage to proceeding this way. It allows me to hold on to the idea that truth is the measure of correctness of belief and assertion. There is a cost, too. It commits me to thinking that the claims other egocentric presentists make about presence are very different from the claims I make about presence. They say that from their point of view certain things are present. I say that certain things are present.

Again this may sound like a grand, radical position. But notice that the claims I make about presence are exactly like the claims other egocentric presentists, from their point of view, make about presence. Suppose Mary and I speak together. From her mouth come the words, "I am female," and from mine come the words, "I am male." Four propositions are involved here:

P   That the one with present experiences is female

P*   That *from Mary's point of view* (the one with present experiences is female)

Q   That the one with present experiences is male

Q*   That *from CJH's point of view* (the one with present experiences is male)

Mary expresses P* and CJH expresses Q. But *From Mary's point of view* (Mary expresses P and CJH expresses Q*). So there is a kind of symmetry between Mary's position and my own.

No Expression

Finally, I could think that Mary does not express a proposition at all. The self-involving utterances of the one with present experiences express propositions, the self-involving utterances of people whose experiences are absent do not. Strictly speaking, Mary does not say anything.

Again, this may seem like a grand and radical thought, but it is not like thinking that Mary is talking gibberish. *From Mary's point of view* (Mary's experiences are present), so *from Mary's point of view* (Mary expresses P), and *from Mary's point of view* (Mary expresses a truth). While there may be no sense in my asking, "What is she saying?" there is perfect sense in my asking, "From her point of view, what is she saying?"

Which of these three options is best? I have a mild preference for the first. The appropriate attitude for an egocentric presentist to take toward the claims of fellow egocentric presentists is: *false, but rightly so.* Indeed, that is the appropriate attitude for *you* to take toward the claims about CJH's metaphysical distinction that fill this very book from cover to cover: false, but rightly so.

You may not share my preference. No matter. Each of the three options gives the egocentric presentist a way of understanding what other egocentric presentists are doing when they use the word "I."[11]

5 A Problem about Personal Identity over Time

Egocentric presentism is not absurd, like the views with which it is easily confused, but its denial is not absurd either. If you are to be persuaded to accept it, then you will need some positive reason for doing so.

Now I take it that I have already given you a positive reason. Egocentric presentism gives us resources to explain why we should, in a robust sense of the word, pay special attention to our own comfort. Egocentric presentists can attend to their comfort by day and enjoy the gentle, untroubled sleep of the righteous by night.

But you may have qualms about settling on a view in metaphysics because you welcome the consequences of believing it. Advocates of this kind of method will say that, when it comes to evaluating a theory in speculative metaphysics, once some minimal standards (of coherence, consistency with empirical evidence, economy, elegance, explanatory efficacy, and such) have been achieved, other factors, including whether it makes sense of what you value, come into play.[1] Opponents will say that this is little better than wishful thinking.

No matter. In the next two chapters I will add another, quite different reason to adopt egocentric presentism: It casts light on otherwise murky questions about personal identity over time. I will argue that egocentric presentists can retain some very appealing views about survival and persistence in unusual cases without committing themselves to a patently indefensible theory of personal identity over time.

5.1 Judgments from the Outside and Inside

Traditional thinking about personal identity over time starts with puzzle cases. You construct such a case by describing, in rich detail, a sequence of events involving people but omitting any mention of personal identity over time, any mention of which person at an earlier time is which person at a later time. The puzzle is then to fill in the unmentioned facts. Who is who?

There are many such cases in the literature (known to the intitiated as "fission," "fusion," "brain swapping," "brain cleaning," "reduplication," etc.). To get the argument going here, we will need to consider one of them. It does not matter very much which we choose. Here is one:

> **A Fantastic Vicissitude** | In the center of an enormous warehouse are two rooms, the interior of one painted egg-yolk yellow, the interior of the other lined with blue velvet. A man is placed in the yellow room and then operated on by a clever but intrusive machine. First the machine scans the man, a process that, sadly, involves subjecting him to a fierce dose of radiation that destroys most of his brain. Then the machine uses the information to create a molecule-for-molecule perfect duplicate of the man fifteen feet away, in the blue room. Then, so as not to allow the original body to go to waste, the machine implants a silicon "brain" into it. Though not very sophisticated, this brain can control the body's vital functions and support a minimal substrate of perceptual experience (think Frankenstein's monster, minus the ability to talk).

Let us call the original person Adam, the silicon-brained person who later lies in the yellow room Sili-Brain, and the person who walks out of the blue room Tele-Product.

Figure 5.1: Adam, Sili-Brain, and Tele-Product

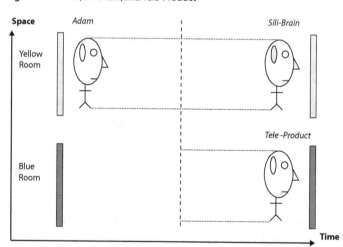

There are two sorts of question you might have about a case like this. First, the traditional question about personal identity over time:

The Question from Outside: Who is who? What happened to Adam?

In response, I am immediately inclined to answer that Adam is Tele-Product. Tele-Product looks like Adam, talks like Adam, says he is Adam. What grounds have I for contradicting him?

Now, maybe some philosophical arguments can persuade me that this is the wrong way of thinking about what happens here. But they can move me only so far. No such arguments will lead me to think Adam is Sili-Brain. Indeed, no such arguments will lead me to think it possible that Adam be Sili-Brain. Whatever the philosopher argues, I will think there is no consistent way of filling in the details of the story according to which Adam is Sili-Brain. Enough has been said, already, to rule out this possibility.

Here is another question:

The Question from Inside: Think yourself into the position of Adam, facing the vicissitude. What is going to happen to you?

When asked this question, I find it natural to think there are different ways in which things might go. When I imagine things going the first way, I imagine all events taking place, physically speaking, in the manner described above, and I imagine staring at yellow walls for a while and then staring at blue walls.

Figure 5.2: One Way for Things to Go

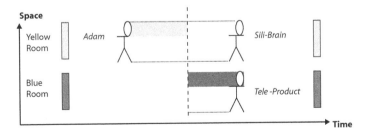

When I imagine things going the second way, I imagine staring at yellow walls for a while . . . and then . . . continuing to stare at yellow walls.

Figure 5.3: A Second Way for Things to Go

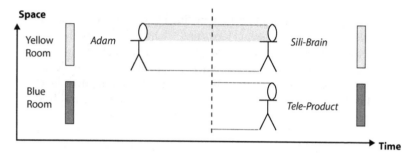

When I imagine things going the third way, I imagine staring at yellow walls for a while . . . and then . . . not having any experiences at all.

Figure 5.4: A Third Way for Things to Go

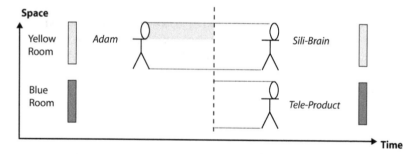

So there are at least three ways in which things might go. And I take it that how I should feel about the upcoming fantastic vicissitude depends very much on the way things will actually go. If, for example, things will go in way two, then I should not feel too bad about the future, even though some nasty, violent things will be happening to my body. If things will go in way three, then I should feel very bad indeed.

These seem like natural responses to the questions from outside and inside. But they give rise to a problem. From the outside I do not regard it as possible that Adam sees yellow after the operation, but from the inside, when I take myself to be Adam, I regard it as possible that *I* might see yellow after the operation. From the outside it seems as if there are limits on what sorts of physical and mental changes Adam can survive, but from the inside, when I take myself to be Adam, it seems as if there are no limits on what sorts of physical and mental changes *I* can survive. As Thomas Nagel puts it:

> When I consider my own individual life from inside, it seems that my existence in the future or the past—the existence of the same 'I' as this one—depends on nothing but itself. To capture my own existence it seems enough to use the word 'I', whose meaning is entirely revealed on any occasion of use. . . .
>
> My nature then appears to be at least conceptually independent not only of bodily continuity but also of all other subjective mental conditions, such as memory and psychological similarity. It can seem, in this frame of mind, that whether a past or future mental state is mine or not is a fact not analyzable in terms of any relations of continuity, psychological or physical, between that state and my present state. The migration of the self from one body to another seems conceivable, even if it is not in fact possible. So does the persistence of the self over a total break in psychological continuity—as in the fantasy of reincarnation without memory.[2]

What picture of the self and of identity through time can make sense of these attractive but seemingly inconsistent judgments from the outside and inside? What picture of the self and of identity over time is such that, if correct, the judgments from the outside and inside both turn out to be right? In the remains of this chapter, I will consider and reject some solutions to this problem.

5.2 Making Sense of Our Judgments from the Outside and Inside

Solution 1: Nonreductionism about Personal Identity over Time

It may appear, prima facie, as if the judgments elicited by asking the question from the inside are judgments about personal identity over time. When I imagine things going the first way, for example, I imagine myself to be a person, Adam, who first sees yellow and then sees blue. And I think it possible that things go this way, so I think it possible that Adam is the same person as Tele-Product. And I think it possible that things go in the second way, so I think it possible that Adam is the same person as Sili-Brain. And I think it possible that things go in the third way, so I think it possible that Adam is neither the same person as Tele-Product nor the same person as Sili-Brain.

To make sense of my seemingly inconsistent judgments, then, our first job is to understand the theory of personal identity that is guiding my judgments from the inside.

Say that a *reductionist* about personal identity over time accepts the following:

(Reductionism)   What it is for A at t_1 to be the same person as B at t_2 is for certain physical or psychological relations to hold between A's body at t_1 and B's body at t_2.[3]

Reductionism is a strong claim. It says, roughly, that facts about personal identity over time are facts about physical and psychological relations between bodies at times. There is a weaker claim in its vicinity:

(Supervenience)   Any possible situations that are the same with respect to physical and psychological relations between bodies at times, are the same with respect to identity over time.

Supervenience says, roughly, that facts about personal identity over time are modally inseparable from facts about physical and psychological relations between bodies at times. Fix all the latter facts and you have fixed the former facts.

Many philosophers who have written about personal identity over time have been at least committed to supervenience. What makes the traditional puzzle cases interesting is the assumption that, by describing a sequence of events in great detail but omitting to mention personal identity over time, you can fix the facts about personal identity over time.

But it looks as if, from the inside, I take both reductionism and supervenience to be false. Tell me as much as you like about the physical and psychological relations between Adam's body, pre-operation, and Sili-Brain and Tele-Product's bodies, post-operation, and I still think that the three possibilities remain open: It might be that I will emerge from the operation looking at the world through Tele-Product's eyes; it might be that I will emerge from the operation looking at the world through Sili-Brain's eyes; it might be that I will not emerge from the operation.

Derek Parfit might agree with this diagnosis of how things seem, from the inside. He has argued, famously, that our commonsense judgments about how and when we survive show that we are in the thrall of a nonreductionist picture of personal identity over time. This picture shapes our attitudes (the petty, undignified ones, for the most part!) toward ourselves and others. And it is incorrect. "We are not what we believe." Once we finally, fully renounce the picture, we will become less selfish, feel less separate from other people, and be rid of our unhealthy preoccupation with our own mortality.[4]

A nonreductionist theory of personal identity could take various forms. According to what has been called the "simple view," facts about identity over time are sui generis.[5] What makes it the case that a person who exists at one time and a person who exists at another are one and the same person? Just the fact that they are one and the same person. What conditions are necessary and sufficient for them to be one and the same? Just that they are one and the same. No more informative analysis can be given. This is not the kind of theory Parfit attributes to us. Rather, he thinks that we think our persistence involves[6] the persistence of "Cartesian egos"—immaterial entities that are associated with[7] particular physical bodies, but not necessarily so. Generally, a person at one time is the same person as a person at another time if and only if the ego associated with the body of the one is the same as the ego associated with the body of the other. So Adam can become Sili-Brain, because Adam's ego can remain associated with Adam's body, even after Adam's original brain has been destroyed. And Adam can become Tele-Product because Adam's ego can cease to be associated with Adam's body and come to be associated with Tele-Product's body.

Does the general public think their own persistence is bound up with the persistence of a Cartesian ego? Maybe Parfit is right. Maybe they do. But if this is offered as an explanation for my judgments from the inside and outside ("you come to these judgments because you accept, deep down, the Cartesian ego picture") then there are reasons to find it unsatisfactory.[8]

First, it is unclear that any nonreductionist view of personal identity over time can really make sense of my judgments from the inside. Suppose we add some talk of immaterial entities to our description of the fantastic vicissitude:

> **The Fantastic Vicissitude** $+$ | .... Furthermore there is an immaterial entity associated with Adam's body, before the operation. It is a *loyal* entity. After the operation it remains associated with that body, now Tele-Product's body.

This does not change my judgments from the inside. I still judge that there are at least three open possibilities, possibilities I distinguish by imagining seeing yellow walls after the operation, imagine seeing blue walls after the operation, and imagining not seeing anything after the operation. So it does not seem right to say that, in the original case, the future seems open to me, because I think that there are three things that might happen to the immaterial entity associated, prior to the operation. The future seems no less open when I know what will happen to that entity.[9]

Second, the Cartesian-ego picture struggles to explain the discrepancy between my judgments from the inside and outside. Why, from the outside, am I not prepared to countenance the possibility that Tele-Product is Adam? If I had internalized a nonreductionist picture of personal identity over time, then you would think I would be more circumspect: "I believe Tele-Product is Adam, but he might not be, because Adam's immaterial ego might have remained associated with Adam's body."

If my judgments from the inside and outside are the fruit of an underlying, consistent metaphysical picture, it is not this one.

Solution 2: Reductionist Indeterminacy about Personal Identity over Time

I said that it would appear, prima facie, as if only a nonreductionist view of personal identity over time could make sense of my judgment (from the inside) that facts about psychological and physical relations between bodies at times do not fix facts about personal identity over time. But there are ways in which, given a reductionist view of personal identity, fixing the facts about physical and psychological relations might fail to fix facts about personal identity. For reductionism is compatible with *indeterminacy*.

An analogy may be instructive here. Imagine a one-hole golf course, SimpleCourse, with a path running across its fairway:

Figure 5.5: SimpleCourse

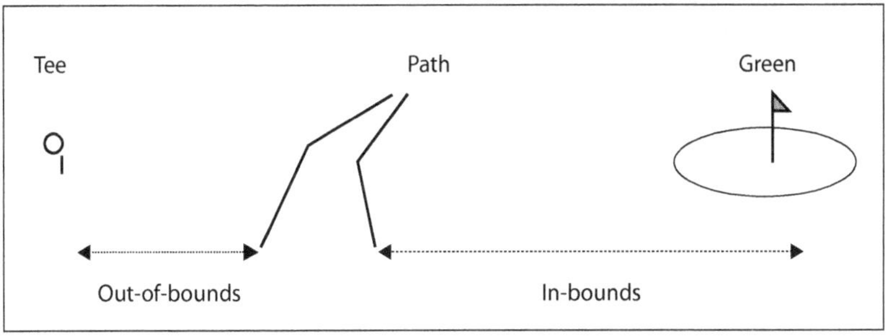

And imagine that the rules for SimpleCourse say:

"All balls that lie ahead of the path are in bounds"

"All balls that lie behind the path are out-of-bounds"

At SimpleCourse, what it is for a ball to be in or out of bounds is for it to be lying at such-and-such a position on the course. Facts about boundedness *reduce*, in the relevant sense, to facts about position. But there are some positions such that for a ball to be lying at that position is for it neither to be determinately in nor determinately out of bounds—a ball on the path, for example:

Figure 5.6: Indeterminacy

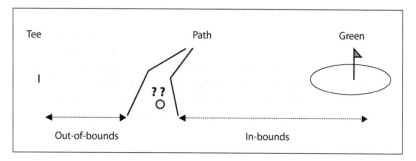

For such a ball, the physical facts about its position do not fix a yes or no answer to the question of whether it is in or out of bounds. There is no fact of the matter as to whether the ball is in or out of bounds.[10]

Are my judgments from the inside guided by the idea that, in a fantastic vicissitude-style case, facts about psychological and physical relations between things do not fix answers to questions about who is who in just this sense? It does not seem so. The natural thing to say about the ball in figure 5.8 is that there is no fact of the matter as to whether it is in or out of bounds. But I do not judge, from the inside, that there is no fact of the matter about whether and how I will survive the fantastic vicissitude. There is a fact, though I may be unsure as to what it is.

So perhaps the guiding theory about personal identity over time is a little more complex. Perhaps it has aspirations to determinacy.

Solution 3: Determinacy-Aspiring, Indeterminate Reductionism

Imagine that SimpleCourse has three rules about boundedness:

"All balls that lie ahead of the path are in bounds"

"All balls that lie behind the path are out of bounds"

"All balls are either in bounds or out of bounds"

If my ball lands on the path I am now in something of a quandary. It must be either in or out of bounds, but which is it? On pain of incoherence, I must extend my ideas about boundedness in some way, perhaps like this:

Figure 5.7: A Mean Extension

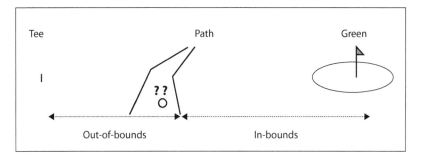

or perhaps like this:

Figure 5.8: A Generous Extension

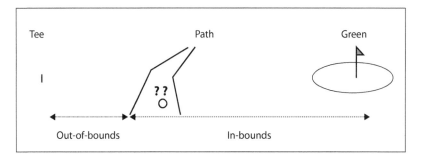

Whichever extension I choose, I can then declare with some authority that the ball is either in or out of bounds.

Some philosophers have proposed a reductionist theory of personal identity over time like this. It determines no matter of fact about who is who in fantastic vicissitude-style cases, but says, nonetheless, that identity is determinate in every case. Faced with such a case, we feel pressure, on pain of incoherence, to extend our theory. Three appropriate extensions might be:

(i) People are *teletransporters.* Their persistence is grounded in psychological continuity and connectedness, not spatiotemporal continuity or token identity of atomic parts. People survive accurate teletransportation.

(ii) People are *human organisms.*

(iii) People are *human beings*—organism-like things that survive iff their brains survive.[11]

If we go with the first extension, then we will conclude that Adam is the same person as Tele-Product. If we go with the second, then we will conclude that Adam is the same person as Sili-Brain. If we go with the third, then we will conclude that Adam is the same person as neither—he ceases to exist when his brain is destroyed. So this might explain, perhaps, why the three scenarios all seem possible to me. They represent the results of extending my theory of personal identity over time in three equally appropriate ways.

Is this really what underlies my judgments from the inside? I think not. For if it were, then there would be no prospective sense in which any of the three appropriate extensions would be right or wrong.[12] But from the inside I judge that one of the three scenarios will come about, and it is not in any way up to me to decide which. If, for example, the second scenario will come about, and I decide to regard myself as a teletransporter, then I will be *making a mistake.*

Solution 4: Ignorance of How People Persist

Perhaps something else is going on. Perhaps, from the inside, I take reductionism about personal identity to be true, so I take it that facts about physical and psychological relations between bodies at times fix facts about who is who in the fantastic vicissitude-style case, but I just do not know what the facts about who is who are. The "possibilities" that I consider open, when I think about the case from the inside, are, on this suggestion, merely epistemic possibilities.

Here is one way for this kind of ignorance to arise: I take it that facts about who is who are determined, in part, by our concept of personal identity over time, but I have not fully grasped the concept. So, if the rules for SimpleCourse are kept in a safe in the clubhouse, I may know that the local concept of boundedness determines a matter of fact about whether my ball is in or out of bounds, but nonetheless need to go back to the safe to find out what this matter of fact is.

Here is another way for the ignorance to arise: I grasp the concept, and know that it determines a matter of fact about who is who, but am unable to apply it to this case. So, if SimpleCourse has the rule:

> "A ball that is behind the space in front of the space behind the space in front of the back edge of the path is not out of bounds."

I may, for want of computing power, just be unable to tell whether my ball is in or out of bounds.

But neither of these can really make sense of my judgments from the inside and out. I do not judge, from the inside, that rigorous conceptual analysis can settle which possibility will arise.

Here is yet another way for this kind of ignorance to arise: I have a firm grip on our concept of a person, and I have no difficulty applying it, but I am ignorant of who is who because I am ignorant of the real nature of persons.

Another analogy should illustrate this thought. Suppose a new radioactive substance—mysterium—has been discovered. Mysterium is locally stable, and large quantities of it have been sent, in sealed crates, to my laboratory for analysis. As my assistants unpack the crates, I say, "Be careful with all this mysterium. It might blow up." I am not thereby saying that mysterium is the kind of substance (like uranium 235 or plutonium) that can blow up if handled in the wrong way. I am saying that for all I know mysterium might have this property. And my ignorance does not stem from my failing to grasp our concept of mysterium, it is not part of our fledgling concept that mysterium blows up or not. My ignorance stems from ignorance of the real nature of the substance.

Thomas Nagel, inspired by Kripke, appealed to this idea to explain our sense, from the inside, that our future is open.[13] When I place myself in Adam's position and wonder about myself and my future, the nature of the thing I am wondering about is not wholly determined by my concept of self. It is in part determined by my concept of self, in part determined by what sorts of things exist in the vicinity of Adam's body. Various candidates exist (an organism, a brain, a heart, etc.), and the thing I am wondering about is the candidate that best satisfies my concept of self. So when I imagine myself to be Adam and judge it possible that I might survive as Sili-Brain, possible that I might survive as Tele-Product, I am taking it that, of all the things in the vicinity of Adam's body, one best satisfies my concept of self, but I do not know its nature.

But this will not do any better at vindicating my judgments from the inside and outside. For one thing, it says that I take there to be a restricted range of candidates in the vicinity of Adam's body (if the range were unrestricted, if there were one thing that survives as Sili-Brain, another that survives as Tele-Product, and another that does not survive, then the nature of the candidate that best satisfies my concept of self would be wholly determined by my concept of self.) It is not obvious to me that I make that assumption. More important, it does not yet explain why there should be a discrepancy between my judgments from the inside and outside. If I take myself to be ignorant of the nature of the thing that best satisfies my concept of *self*, when I think about Adam's situation from the inside, why do I not take myself to be ignorant of the nature of the thing that best satisfies my concept of *Adam the person* when I think about Adam's situation from the outside?

5.3 Error Theories

If any of the above proposals are correct, then some of my judgments from the outside and inside are incorrect: I am making a mistake. In one sense, then, these proposals do not explain my judgments from the outside and inside. But you might think that this does not tell against the proposals. Maybe I am indeed making a mistake, and the proposals can shed light on what it is.

Maybe, for example, Parfit is broadly right, but I have contradictory beliefs. My judgments from the outside and inside both concern personal identity over time, but I have internalized two different pictures of personal identity over time, reductionist and nonreductionist. And for some reason thinking about cases from the outside prompts me to wheel out the reductionist picture, whereas thinking about cases from the inside triggers me to wheel out the nonreductionist picture.

Or maybe, for another example, Nagel is broadly right, but I am mistaken about whether there is a thing that satisfies my concept of *Adam the person* when I think about Adam's situation from the outside.

The different proposals will then amount to different versions of an *error theory*, according to which attractive patterns of thought are the product of confusions of one kind or other. I have nothing in principle against error theories. Philosophy would be rather dull if we never allowed sustained reflection to cast doubt on our prereflective judgments. But before we embrace an error theory, we should pause and consider whether there is a more charitable interpretation of the judgments in question. In this case, I think there is.

6 The Solution

Before we get to the right way to make sense of our judgments from the outside and inside, let us consider one more explanation, due to Dilip Ninan.[1] I think that Ninan's explanation does not quite work, but it gets one important thing right, and the way in which it does not quite work is instructive.

6.1 Judgments from the Inside Do Not Concern Personal Identity over Time

First suppose a generous material ontology. Suppose in particular that there are three overlapping things in Adam's vicinity before the operation. These three things are physically just the same before the operation. They have all the same boundaries, all the same parts (a heart, a pair of lungs, fingers, toes, a carbon-based brain, etc.), all the same temporary features, but they suffer different fates. One of them, call it "Jumps," moves to the blue room mid-operation. Another, call it "Stays," stays in the yellow room before, during and after the operation. Another, call it "Stops," ceases to exist mid-operation.[2]

Here, shaded in gray, are the chunks of space-time carved out by each of the three creatures, as they undergo the operation:

Figure 6.1: Where Are Jumps, Stays, and Stops?

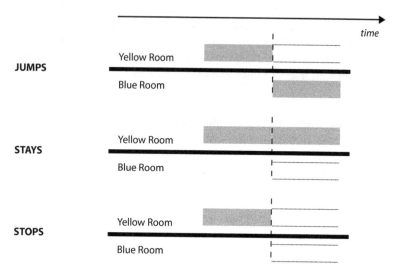

Next suppose that, prior to the operation, each of these things is having experiences, and experiences of the same kind. Next suppose that only one of these things, Jumps, is a person. Why? Because the psychological approach to personal identity over time is broadly correct. Finally, suppose that names like "Adam" and "Tele-Product" refer to people.

Supposing all this, my judgments from the outside make perfect sense. When, before the operation, I use "Adam" to refer to the person in the yellow room, I am referring to Jumps. Stays and Stops are not people, so Jumps is the only person around. When, after the operation, I use "Tele-Product" to refer to the person in the blue room, I am again referring to Jumps. Jumps is, again, the only person around. So I am right to judge that Adam is Tele-Product. And I am right to judge it impossible that Adam survive in the yellow room. Adam is a person and people cannot undergo psychological changes as abrupt and radical as those suffered by Stays.

My judgments from the inside make perfect sense, too. When I imagine myself in the yellow room, before the operation, I imagine myself to be in an unusual kind of situation. Here I am, morosely inspecting the lurid walls, and I know that there are three creatures—Stays, Jumps, and Stops—having experiences qualitatively just like the ones I am having. But, just as in the "after the train crash" case (in which I know there are two creatures—Joe Bloggs and CJH—having experiences qualitatively just like the ones I am having), there is something I do not know. I do not know who I am. There are three salient epistemic possibilities: I could be Stays, Jumps, or Stops. So I could be the thing that will be in the yellow room, post-operation, the thing that will be in the blue room, post-operation, or the thing that will cease to exist, mid operation. So I am right to judge, from the inside, that there are three open possibilities concerning who I will be.

Ninan's project has several virtues. First, it is aiming at the right target. It is trying to make sense of the discrepancy between my judgments from the outside and inside. Second, it gives the right kind of diagnosis of my judgments from the inside. They do not concern personal identity over time. When I judge it possible that I will be lying in the yellow room after the operation, I am not implicitly assuming a view of personal identity over time according to which it is an open possibility that Adam, the person, will be lying in the yellow room after the operation. Third, its foundational suppositions—a generous material ontology and a broadly Lockean theory of personal identity over time—are not so exotic and arcane as to render it doomed from the outset.

But I think it still does not do the job we want done, which is to vindicate my judgments from the outside and in, because I think that if the theory is right, my judgments from the inside are mistaken.[3] If I find myself in Adam's position before the operation, and know there are three temporarily coincident creatures in my vicinity—Stays, Jumps, and Stops—then it is a mistake for me to think that I am ignorant about which of them I really am, because it is a mistake for me to think that there is an unknown fact of the matter about which of them I really am. It is not always true that, when two things are having experiences qualitatively just like mine, there is an unknown fact of the matter about which of them I really am.

I find this intuitively obvious. Supposing that I discover that two temporarily co-extensive creatures share all of my present parts, there is something wrongheaded about the question "Which of them am I, really?" But you may not.[4] So, to give some flesh to the intuition, I will sketch out a picture of what ignorance concerning myself but not the world, so called "de se ignorance," involves.

6.2 De Se Ignorance

The basic idea is that, when I know a great deal about what the world is like but do not know who I am, in the "after the train crash" case, for example, and I ask, "Who am I? Am I CJH or Joe Bloggs?" I am asking a *linking question*. Here is a typical linking question: I have two maps of the Rocky Mountains. Map 1 covers the whole range in all of its crumbling glory. Map 2 covers only the southern portion of the range. Pointing in turn at each map I ask:

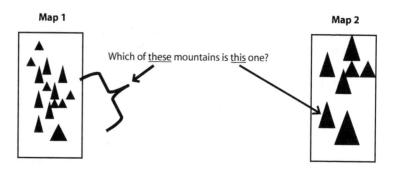

I call this is a linking question because, loosely speaking, I want to know how to link up the maps. There are a couple of more precise ways to think about what I am asking. One is to think of the maps as containing representations of mountains and to think of my question as concerning representations of mountains. When I gesture at map 1 and say "these mountains," I pick out a collection of triangles on map 1. When I gesture at map 2 and say "this one," I pick out a single triangle on map 2. What I want to know is which of the specified collection of triangles on map 1 represents the mountain that is represented by the specified triangle on map 2.

Another more precise way to think about the question is to think of the maps as devices that enable me to refer to, and think about, mountains. When I gesture at map 2, I pick out a mountain. I want to know how to use map 1 to pick out that very mountain. (Furthermore, the way I phrase the question—"Which of *these* mountains"—indicates that I already have a rough idea about how to do so: by pointing somewhere within the bottom half of the map.)

For present purposes we do not need to decide which way of thinking about linking questions is the right one, or even whether they are in competition with one another. I suspect that, for the most part, they are not.

Linking questions need not involve maps. Here is another linking question: I have a map of the Rocky Mountains, covering the whole range in all its crumbling glory, and a photograph of a mountain. Pointing in turn at the map and the photograph, I ask:

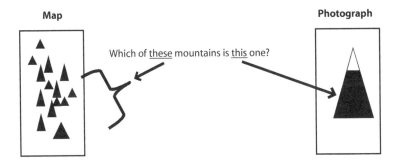

And here is another linking question: I have what you might call an "objective mental picture" of the Rocky Mountain Range: I have ideas about how many mountains there are, about what they are called, about their sizes, about their locations, and so forth. And I have what you might call a "perspectival mental picture" of a snowcapped mountain: because I am standing in front of such a mountain, in the middle of a clear day, with my well-functioning eyes open, and nothing between me and it. And I ask:

'Objective Picture'   **'Perspectival Picture'**

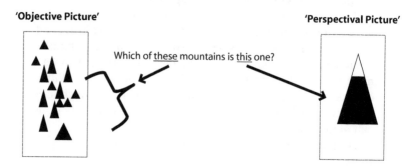

Which of <u>these</u> mountains is <u>this</u> one?

This is clearly a different sort of linking question. The talk of pictures is at best crudely metaphorical. There are no maps or photographs inside my brain. So it is not very helpful to think about this question the first way: to think that I am gesturing, first at some triangles on my objective mental picture (something like an *inner map*), then at a looming triangle on my perspectival mental picture (something like an *inner photograph*), and asking which of the former represents the mountain represented by the latter.

But it remains helpful to think about the question the second way. I have different devices for picking out things in the world. One device involves perception—I pick things out by sensing them (*that* mountain, *that* smell, *that* sound.) But there are many others. I may pick out things by naming them, by cataloguing their intrinsic or extrinsic properties, by remembering them, by pointing at representations of them, and so forth. In this context, when I gesture at the mountain before me I use my senses to pick out a mountain. And I want to know how to pick out that mountain in other ways—by naming it, cataloguing its properties, locating it within my "mental picture" of the Rocky Mountain range . . . and so forth.

When I ask "Who am I?" in a case like the "after the train crash" case, you might think I am asking a similar sort of linking question. There is something that I pick out by sensing it: *me*. And I want to know how to pick out that thing in other ways, by naming it, describing its location in the hospital, and so forth. Metaphorically, then, it is as if I am asking:

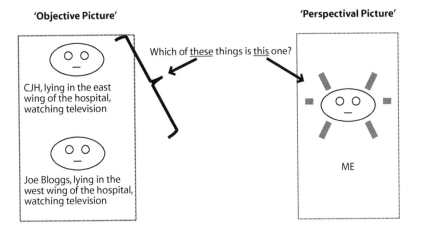

'Objective Picture'
'Perspectival Picture'

Which of <u>these</u> things is <u>this</u> one?

CJH, lying in the east wing of the hospital, watching television

Joe Bloggs, lying in the west wing of the hospital, watching television

ME

But this will not work as a general account of de se ignorance. For one thing, it suggests that I sense myself, whenever I wonder who I am. But that does not seem right. When I wonder who I am while lying on my back and looking up at the sky, I see, feel, and hear many things—clouds, grass, a passing airplane—but I do not see, hear, or feel myself. For another thing, it cannot explain why I may wonder of anything I sense whether it is me. It cannot explain, for example, why I may wonder, looking across at the mirror during a packed ballet class, whether *that* pathetically weak and inflexible excuse for a human being is me. It does not seem right to say of such cases that I am picking something out by sensing it, and wondering how to pick out that very thing by name, description, and so forth. I am not interested in what that weedy guy's name is. I am not interested in how to describe him. He's weedy, I can see that. I am interested in whether he is me.

Better to say that, when I ask "Who am I?" in a case like the "after the train crash" case, I am asking a different kind of linking question. There are many things I pick out by sensing them, call them my *perceptual objects* (seemingly: a television set, a plaster-encased foot, two lights on the ceiling[5]) and I want to know how to pick out, in other ways, the thing that has all these things as perceptual objects. Metaphorically it is as if I am asking:

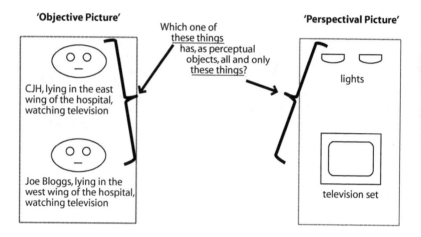

And the proper answer to the question is, of course, "CJH." Because CJH, and not Joe Bloggs, has those lights and that television set as perceptual objects.

In the ballet class, when I ask "Which of those things in the mirror is *me*?" or "Is that pathetic thing me?" there are many things that I sense, and I am wondering how to pick out, by sensing and attending, the thing that has all of those things as perceptual objects. Metaphorically, it is as if I am asking:

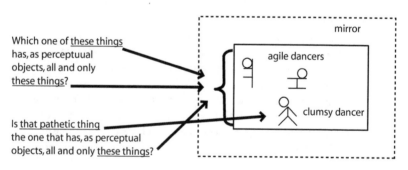

Generally, when I ask 'Who am I?' there are many things I sense, and I want to know how to pick out, in some implicitly specified way (it may be by sensing and pointing, by sensing and attending, by naming, by describing, or by locating on a map), the thing that has all and only the sensed things as perceptual objects.

This seems to me an attractive picture of ignorance concerning oneself.[6] I would add a significant tweak: The things I sense are present. So when I ask "Who am I?" I want to know how to pick out, in some implicitly specified way, the thing that has all and only present things as perceptual objects.[7] You may not accept the tweak. No matter, for present purposes.

In any case, if even the untweaked picture is right then, if I find myself in Adam's position pre-operation, and realize that there are indeed many temporarily co-extensive things sharing my present parts, there is no sense in my asking "Who am I, Stays, Jumps, or Stops?" To ask that is to ask "Which one of Stays, Jumps, and Stops has all and only these sensed things (the yellow walls, etc.[8]) as perceptual objects?" But Stays, Jumps, and Stops have all the same perceptual objects. If any of them have all and only these things as perceptual objects, then they all do.

But, on Ninan's account, I do take there to be sense in the question "Who am I, Stays, Jumps, or Stops?" So Ninan's account does not vindicate my judgments from the inside. If Ninan is right then, from the inside, I judge things to be possible that really are not.

6.3 The Solution

Again, it could be that Ninan is broadly right and that my judgments from the inside are the product of a blunder: I am mistakenly prone to think that, whenever several entities are presently having experiences just like mine, there must be a fact of the matter as to which of them really is me. But there is a more generous explanation of the judgments from outside and inside, one that vindicates them both.

Let us consider what an egocentric presentist should say about how presence is distributed across possible states of affairs and across time. As an egocentric presentist, I believe that CJH alone has present experiences. This does not just mark him out among his contemporaries. It marks him out among all the people who have ever been or will ever be.

Is it necessary that CJH be the one with present experiences? The natural thing to say is no. I can vividly imagine a scenario in which, for example, Ralph Nader is the one with present experiences. Indeed, that is precisely what I do when I try to "see the world through Ralph Nader's eyes" and imagine being him. It is actually the case that *from Ralph Nader's point of view* (Ralph Nader's experiences are present). I imagine that, contrary to fact, Ralph Nader's experiences are present. On this view what I am imagining is a real metaphysical possibility, a way that things might have been. When I say "thank goodness I am not Ralph Nader," I am thanking goodness for the fact that things are the way they actually are, rather than this other way they might have been.

So "the one with present experiences" (the term "I" stands for) is a definite description that is satisfied by different things in different possible states of affairs. So, like all such descriptions, it behaves as a *modally nonrigid referring term.*[9]

Given that "I" is modally nonrigid, when I am assessing de se modal claims (claims like "I could have been Nader"), it will pay to bear in mind that modally nonrigid referring terms have one very important feature. To put it in an abstract way: Where "t" is such a term, and "φ" is an open formula, and "M" is a modal operator, it does not always follow from

1. $M(\varphi(t))$

that

2. $\exists x(x = t\ (M(\varphi(x))))$

For example, it does not follow from

1. It could have been the case that I was born in Connecticut, to the Naders.

that

2. There is someone who is me, and it could have been the case that he was born in Connecticut, to the Naders.

Yes it could have been that Ralph Nader, son of the Naders, was the one with present experiences. No, the one with present experiences, CJH, could not have been son of the Naders.

Is it necessary that only one person ever have present experiences? Again, the natural thing to say is no. Egocentric presentism gives me conceptual resources to imagine being one sentient creature and then, later, being another sentient creature. So (recall Nagel's "fantasy of reincarnation without memory") I can imagine that, after a lifetime of oblivious egg consumption, I die a happy philosopher, then find myself in a cage eighteen inches tall by twelve inches wide, my beak clipped to its base. This need not involve imagining that CJH dies a happy philosopher and then becomes a battery chicken. It may only involve imagining that after CJH's death there are again present experiences, and they are the experiences of a battery chicken. Once again this is a real, real nasty, metaphysical possibility.

So "the one with present experiences" is a definite description that may be satisfied by different things at different times. Like all such descriptions, it behaves as a *temporally nonrigid referring term*.

Given that "I" is temporally nonrigid, when I am assessing de se tensed claims (like "I will be happy soon"), it will pay to bear in mind that temporally nonrigid referring terms have a similar important feature. Where "t" is such a term and "φ" is an open formula and "T" is a tensed operator, it does not always follow from

1. $T(\varphi(t))$

that

2. $\exists x(x = t \ (T(\varphi(x))))$

For example, it does not follow from

1. It will be the case that I am a battery chicken.

that

2. There is someone who is me, and it will be the case that he is a battery chicken.

Yes, in the dread scenario of reincarnation without memory, it will be the case, after CJH's body has been consumed by worms, that the one with present experiences is a battery chicken. No, CJH will not be a battery chicken.

In light of this, look back at my judgments from the inside. What do I do when I consider, for example, scenario one a live possibility and imagine it coming about?

Figure 6.8: Scenario One Revisited

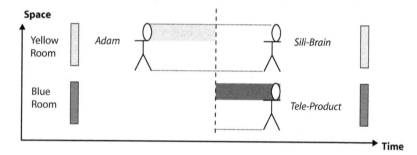

In considering scenario one a live possibility, I consider it possible (and rightly so) that initially Adam's experiences are present, and then, after the operation, Tele-Product's experiences are present. In imagining it coming about, I imagine first staring at yellow walls and then staring at blue walls. This need only involve imagining present yellow-wall staring and then imagining present blue-wall staring. It need not involve imagining anything at all about personal identity over time, about who is who.

But you can see why my judgments from the inside about which experiences might be present are easily confused with judgments about who might be who. If I find myself in Adam's position, in scenario one, I would be right to think:

1.   It will be the case that I am Tele-Product.

from which it may seem to follow that:

2.   I am somebody such that it will be the case that he is Tele-Product.

which, together with

3.   I am Adam.

would seem to imply

4.   Adam will be Tele-Product.

So it might seem as if, in judging scenario one possible, I am judging it possible that Adam be Tele-Product. But this is not right.
Since "I" is a temporally nonrigid referring term, it is a mistake to
infer 2 from 1. It does not follow from the fact that it will be the
case that Tele-Product is the one with present experiences, that
the one with present experiences (Adam) will be Tele-Product.
Yes, Tele-Product will be me. No, I will not be Tele-Product.

In sum: If egocentric presentism is correct, then my judgments
from the inside are correct, and they do not concern personal
identity over time.

But, although egocentric presentism says nothing about people
and about how they persist, I think I do have some independent
views about this matter. In particular, I am inclined to think that
people are wholly physical things, with persistence conditions
given by some form of a reductionist psychological approach to
personal identity over time. That inclination is reflected in my
judgments from the outside—I judge that Adam cannot survive
as Sili-Brain. But there is no tension between these judgments
and my judgments from the inside.

This is *not* to say that we are all secretly egocentric presentists,
that if the person in the street shares my judgments from inside
and outside, it is because he or she is, without knowing it, combining egocentric presentism with a reductionist view of personal
identity over time. I do not have much of an idea of what the person in the street thinks, nor, for these purposes, do I care. Maybe
many people in the street are confused about personal identity
over time. Maybe they sometimes apply a reductionist theory,
sometimes a nonreductionist theory. No matter.

It is to say, rather, that egocentric presentism offers you a way
to reconcile some attractive intuitions about anticipation and
survival with theoretical commitments to a reductionist view of
personal identity over time. If you do not share the intuitions or
the commitments, this may not interest you. But if, like me, you

have them, then you should take this to be a strong mark in its favor.

6.4 Dread, Existential and Anticipatory

When we think about the future, two things, among many others, matter to us a great deal. First, there is *being around*. The prospect of the alternative, not being around, fills us with a special kind of dread, fairly described as existential. Second, there is *being comfortable*. The prospect of being in pain fills us with a different kind of dread, fairly described as anticipatory.

Parfit has a revisionary slogan: "Identity is not what matters. What matters is psychological continuity and connectedness." He thinks it revisionary because he thinks that most of us have a black-or-white attitude to the future. Our concern for being around amounts to a concern that there be, in future, a person who bears the on-or-off relation of personal identity to ourselves now. And our concern for not being in pain amounts to a concern that the experiences of this person be pleasant. But, says Parfit, once you fully understand the truth about personal identity over time, you will see that you should think about the future in shades of gray. You should be more or less satisfied to the extent that there exist future people who are more or less strongly psychologically continuous with and connected to you now. You should be more or less troubled by future pleasures and pains to the extent that the people who have them are more or less strongly psychologically continuous with and connected to you now. Your anticipatory and existential feelings about the future should not behave like a light governed by a switch. They should behave like a light governed by a dimmer.

I have a different slogan: "Identity is not what matters, what matters is who will be me." I am very fond of many people, including CJH, and I want all those people to survive and prosper. But my bare concern for being around amounts only to a concern that there be present experiences in future. Facing a dangerous vicissitude, I ask, "After this is over, will someone be me?" And my anticipatory concern amounts to special concern for the hedonic quality of future present experiences. Facing a future in which many people suffer, I ask, "Will I suffer?" Though I know myself to be CJH, these are not quite the same questions as "After this is over, will someone be CJH?" and "Will CJH suffer?" because it is at best a contingent truth that CJH always, alone, has present experiences.

Why should I exhibit this pattern of concern? Because it matters simpliciter that there be present experiences in future and that they be good. Worlds in which there continue to be present experiences (of a certain kind, at least) are, all other things being equal, better than worlds in which presence is a thing of the past. The quality of present experiences makes a greater contribution to the value of a world than the quality of absent experiences. So, as an egocentric presentist, I take it that my pattern of concern is consistent with, and supported by, considerations of the greater good.

As Parfit makes clear, if I did not accept egocentric presentism, it might seem a bit of a mystery as to why I should have special concern for what will happen to me. To fix ideas: Let us say that I am to suffer a dental operation tomorrow, and there will be no fantastic vicissitudes in the meantime. Why should I be especially concerned about my suffering tomorrow, rather than about the suffering of those thousands of other people who will suffer dental operations tomorrow?

Some philosophers think that when I ask "Should I have special concern for my suffering tomorrow?" the "I" picks out a thing that is strictly speaking identical with the thing that suffers tomorrow. The challenge for these philosophers is to explain why a thing should have special concern for its own comfort. As I have argued in the first three chapters, an egocentric presentist is peculiarly well equipped to meet this challenge. I will not rehearse the argument here.

Other philosophers think that the "I" picks out a thing that is not strictly speaking identical with the thing that suffers tomorrow. The "I" picks out what they call a person stage, a thing that exists for (at best) a very brief period of time. The thing that suffers is a distinct person stage. The relation that obtains between them is some identity surrogate (e.g., the relation that obtains between two parts of one four-dimensionally extended thing).[10] Let us call the thing that the "I" picks out $PS_{Worrier}$ and the thing that suffers $PS_{Sufferer}$. The challenge for these philosophers is to explain why $PS_{Worrier}$ should have special concern for the suffering of $PS_{Sufferer}$, given that they are distinct things. Some observations these philosophers have made are:

(Empathy) Because $PS_{Sufferer}$ is psychologically similar to $PS_{Worrier}$, $PS_{Worrier}$ can empathize in an especially vivid way with his pain. $PS_{Worrier}$ can imagine especially clearly what it will be like.[11]

(Reliable Executor) Because $PS_{Sufferer}$ is psychologically similar to $PS_{Worrier}$, he is more likely to satisfy $PS_{Worrier}$'s future-oriented desires, and to work toward the success of $PS_{Worrier}$'s long-term projects.[12]

(Dependence) Because $PS_{Sufferer}$'s psychology is counterfactually dependent on $PS_{Worrier}$'s in various intimate ways, he will experience the pain in the wake of $PS_{Worrier}$'s thinking about it. His experience of the pain will be shaped by $PS_{Worrier}$'s anticipation of it.[13]

But none of these observations does a very good job of justifying special concern for $PS_{Sufferer}$'s pain. In response to (Empathy): Pain is pain. While there may be a vast difference between your experiences when you sigh at the sight of a sunset and mine when I do the same thing, it seems plausible to imagine that having teeth drilled feels pretty much the same to everyone. In response to (Reliable Executor): Whether $PS_{Sufferer}$ suffers mildly or severely on the dentist's chair typically has no bearing on whether $PS_{Worrier}$'s future-oriented desires will be satisfied (except, perhaps, for a desire on his part that things psychologically continuous with me not suffer—but the justification for that desire is precisely what is at issue.) In response to (Dependence): It may be that $PS_{Worrier}$ has a special kind of control over the manner in which $PS_{Sufferer}$ will suffer, and that may give $PS_{Worrier}$ a special kind of responsibility for $PS_{Sufferer}$'s suffering, but it is very hard to see why that responsibility would justify special concern.

PS_{Worrier} is unlikely to make PS_{Sufferer}'s experience any better by fretting about it. Fretting usually makes such things worse.

An egocentric presentist's answer is simpler and, I think, more persuasive. No matter whether I am strictly speaking identical with the thing that will suffer tomorrow, I should be especially concerned about his suffering because it will be present.

7 Skepticism and Humility

I will close on the defensive, by addressing two clusters of worries that tend to arise when people take egocentric presentism seriously. The first worries have to do with the epistemology of presence. Broadly: How do we know what is present? The second worries have to with humility. Broadly: Is it not distasteful to think yourself special?

7.1 Skepticism

Here is one skeptical worry. You might wonder about whether egocentric presentists are entitled to believe their own experiences are present. You might urge me to ask myself some questions: "What grounds do I have for believing that there are monadically present things? Would I not believe the same even if there were no such things? And, even if I have grounds for believing that there are present things, what grounds do I have for believing that they are the perceptual objects of CJH? Would CJH not believe that his perceptual objects were present even if Barack Obama's perceptual objects were present, even if I were Barack Obama?"

The questions should not trouble an egocentric presentist very much. Recall the Cartesian thought process that leads me to egocentric presentism. At the very first stage of the process, one thing is evident:

(E1)   *That some things (whatever their nature) are present*

By the second stage of the process, another thing is evident:

(E2)   *That the present things are perceptual objects of CJH*

I could be tempted, at some later stage in the process, to take a revisionist view of the evidence given to me at the first and second stages of the process. I could be tempted to think that the evidence given to me at the first stage of the process was:

(E1*)   *That CJH stands in a certain relation to some things (whatever their nature): the relation of taking them to be present*

and the evidence given to me at the second stage of the process was:

(E2*)   *That the things CJH takes to be present are his own perceptual objects*

If I succumbed to this temptation, I could reasonably worry, "What grounds do I have for inferring (E1) from my real evidence, (E1*)? What grounds do I have for inferring that some things are present from the evident fact that CJH takes some things to be present? After all, CJH would take some things to be present even if nothing were present." And I could reasonably worry, "What grounds do I have for inferring (E2) from my real evidence, (E2*)? What grounds do I have for inferring that CJH's perceptual objects are present from the evident fact that the things CJH takes to be present are his own perceptual objects? After all, CJH would take his own perceptual objects to present even if they were not."

But to succumb to the temptation would be to recast the egocentric presentist's foundational insight (that some things are present) in relational terms (that some things bear certain relation to a person), and this is precisely what egocentric presentists refuse to do. It is their refusal to do this that makes them egocentric presentists.

Here is another skeptical worry. You might wonder whether egocentric presentists are entitled to believe their own experiences have been and will be present. You might urge me to ask myself some further questions: Given that it is possible that presence flits around like a butterfly, given that it is possible, for example, that it rested on the head of Barack Obama yesterday, rests on the head of CJH today, and will rest on the head of Mick Jagger tomorrow, what grounds do I have for thinking that presence sticks with CJH?

Let us address the past component of the question first: What grounds do I have for thinking that CJH's experiences *were* present, yesterday, say? How do I know that CJH's experiences have not become present just recently?

These questions seem analogous to questions that some philosophers suppose to be troubling for the view that mental facts (in particular facts about consciousness and what it is like to have different kinds of experiences) do not metaphysically supervene on physical facts. It may be obvious to me now that there is something is it is like for me to stare at a green light, but how do I know that this is not what it was like for me to stare at a red thing yesterday (call this inner spectrum inversion)? It may be obvious to me now that I am conscious, but how do I know that I was not unconscious yesterday?

One line of response is to say, "I know these things have not happened because I would have noticed if they had. If my inner spectrum had inverted, I would have started running through traffic lights, mistaking the sky for the ground and the ground for the sky, confusing autumn with spring, and generally behaving in an unstable way. If I had suddenly become conscious, I would have been overwhelmed by the vivid texture of my experiences. But I have been neither confused nor overwhelmed."

The analogous response in this case, "I know my experiences have not suddenly become present because I would have noticed if they had" is not very satisfactory. I will accept the counterfactual only if I accept that there are *bridging laws*, laws that would preclude presence flitting about like a butterfly.[1] But what grounds do I have for believing that there are such laws? I cannot appeal to induction from the past, because the first step, "in the past, presence has never flitted about, unnoticed," is precisely what is in question.

A better response harkens back, once again, to the Cartesian thought process that gets egocentric presentism going. At the second stage of the process, (E2) is evident. But does (E2) concern how things are or how things have been? Is it

(E2₁)   *that CJH has, and has had, present experiences*

or

(E2$_2$) *that CJH has present experiences, and has memories as of having had present experiences?*

If it is the latter then I can reasonably ask myself, "What grounds do I have for inferring that CJH has had present experiences, from his having memories as of having had present experiences? After all, CJH would have memories as of having had present experiences even if he never had present experiences." But is it the latter? This is a delicate question. How one answers it will depend on whether one thinks that, if one is in the business of justifying beliefs by appeal to evident truths, one's beliefs at a time can be justified only by appeal to truths that are evident *at that time*— that I now have such-and-such perceptions, that I now have such-and-such memories, etc. I am inclined to think not. If, during a period of introspection, someone asks me what grounds I have for believing that CJH's experiences of ten minutes ago were present, I am entitled to appeal not merely to its being evident that CJH has memories as of having present experiences ten minutes ago, but also to its having been evident ten minutes ago that CJH had present experiences then. I am entitled to say, "it has been evident over a period of time that CJH has present experiences." And that suffices as a response to the question "What grounds do I have for believing that, in the past, CJH's experiences have been present?"

What about the future, then? What grounds do I have for believing that, in the future, CJH's experiences will be present? I say *induction*. In the past CJH's experiences have been present, so I am entitled to think they will remain so. What is the precise form of the general law that applies here? Precisely what mechanism secures presence as time goes by? I do not know. Given that the history of CJH is less than exotic, his experiences having been present is consistent with presence-tracking spatiotemporal continuity, psychological continuity, and many other things beside. Indeed, it may be that there is no general law to know about. Consider a case in which spatiotemporal continuity and psychological continuity come apart:

Psychology Swapping | CJH and Ralph Nader swap psychologies. All of Ralph Nader's beliefs, desires, and mental capabilities are implanted in CJH's body. All of CJH's beliefs, desires, and mental capabilities are implanted in Ralph Nader's body.

Visually:

Figure 7.1: Will I Be Nader?

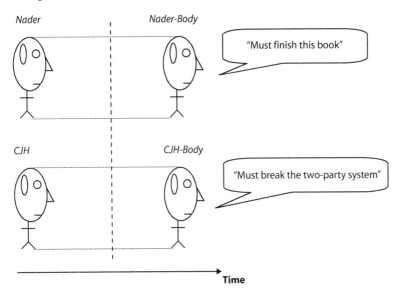

It may be that there is no fact of the matter about what would happen if I were CJH and things were to pan out like this. It may be that the counterfactual

C1   "If I were to submit to the psychology swap, then either Nader-Body would later be me or CJH-Body would later be me."

is true, but the counterfactuals

C2   "If I were to submit to the psychology swap, then Nader-Body would later be me."

C3   "If I were to submit to the psychology swap, then CJH would later be me."

are not. Why? Think about the counterfactuals in broadly Lewisian terms. Since I will not actually undergo a psychology swap, to evaluate the counterfactuals I must consider the saliently closest class of non-actual possible worlds in which I do undergo a psychology swap and see who, in those worlds, has present experiences after the big event. But it may be that, all other things being equal, worlds in which Nader-Body has present experiences (worlds in which presence tracks psychological continuity) are not saliently closer than worlds in which CJH-Body has present experiences (worlds in which presence tracks spatiotemporal continuity.)

But in our world, a world that is sadly devoid of basic teletransportation and brain transplantation technology, this is rather beside the point. The point is that I am entitled to believe that presence will remain with CJH in future.

7.2 Humility

Here is a different kind of worry: What spectacular hubris! The universe is very large indeed. Cosmologists estimate that its observable part measures around ninety-three billion light years in diameter, and contains around 10^{22} stars, while the size of its unobservable part is, literally speaking, unfathomable. What kind of a person, in the face of such immensity, would cling to the thought that there is something radically unique about our star and its third planet—in that they alone play host to presence?

And, for that matter, though the Earth may be twenty orders of magnitude smaller than the observable universe, it is pretty big, too. Population scientists estimate that around ninety-six billion people have ever lived on it. What kind of a person, in the face of such a multitude, would cling to the thought that there is something radically unique about himself—in that he alone has present experiences?

Someone very arrogant indeed.

I find it difficult to address this worry in a clean way, because I am not entirely sure about what is motivating it. I see at least two things that may be going in the worrier's mind.

In the 1970s Weetabix Ltd., the makers of Ready Brek, an instant hot cereal, based an advertising campaign on the slogan "Get up and Glow." A typical TV ad would open with a camera, fitted with a blue lens for dramatic effect, panning across a street on a frigid January morning. Crowds of children, hunkering down into their duffel coats, would be walking to school. But one would stick out, the one whose responsible parents fed him hot cereal for breakfast, the "Ready Brek kid." He would be enveloped in an intense orange glow.

I suspect that some worriers take it that the egocentric presentist, absurdly, thinks of himself as a sort of Ready Brek kid. Around one innocuous little person in one innocuous little corner of the vast and splendid universe, there is a sort of glow, a glow that is radically unlike anything to be found elsewhere, a glow that bestows a special significance on its bearer.

If this is what underlies the worry, then it is based on another misunderstanding of the view. Being present is nothing at all like glowing (or being orange, or being big, and so forth). To imagine that a thing is present, you need only imagine perceiving it. And having present experiences is nothing at all like being surrounded by a glow. To imagine that someone has present experiences, you need only imagine that her perceptual objects are present, which need only involve imagining perceiving what she perceives.

To put the point another way, you will not get a grasp of how the egocentric presentist takes things to be by picturing the world and all it contains, including him, third-personally, and then adding something to your third-personal picture—a dab of luminescent paint, metaphorically speaking. To get a grasp of how he takes things to be you need to imagine being him, in the world.

I suspect that other worriers are moved by a visceral moralism: When many, many other people's lives are intimately connected with your own, there is disvirtue in believing that your pleasures and pains are special, and there's an end on it!

Maybe so. But there is virtue in integrity. It is true that an egocentric presentist will be an egocentric hedonist to some greater or lesser degree, but pretty much all of us, visceral moralists included, are egocentric hedonists to some greater or lesser degree—we feel, desire, and behave as if our own pleasures and pains are to some greater or lesser degree special. I find it hard to see how, when two people both feel, desire, and behave as if something were the case, the person who does not believe it to be the case can claim to occupy higher moral ground than the person who does.

7.3 Wrapping Up

I am sure that I have not addressed every reasonable objection against, or worry about, egocentric presentism. But I hope, just now and in chapter four, to have given you a sense of now egocentric presentists might respond to various kinds of objections, of the resources available to them. If you have residual concerns, they must be balanced against the considerable advantages of the view. By way of wrapping up, let me repeat what these are.

First, the centerpiece of egocentric presentism is *the most obvious thing in the world*: One person, alone, has experiences that are in one important respect radically unlike the experiences of anybody else.

Second, egocentric presentism gives substance to the attractive thought that a full specification of the physical facts can leave it open whether a particular future person will be *me*, without commitment to a nonreductionist view of personal identity over time.[2]

Third, egocentric presentism is uniquely capable of making sense of why we should all be mild egocentric hedonists. Each person's mild egocentric hedonism tracks what is valuable simpliciter.[3]

Whether you accept the view will (and I think *should*) come down, not to intricate questions in epistemology, but to whether you can stomach the implications of this third advantage. When one's life goes well, it is gratifying to discover that one is special. But when it goes badly, there may be solace in the thought that the troubles of one little person don't amount to a hill of beans in this crazy world.

Notes

Introduction
1. Hume (1739), book 1, chapter 4, section 6.
2. Homer, *The Illiad*, book XXI, line 161.
3. Ibid., Book XVI, line 283.
4. Section 4.4 of this book.
5. Section 3.4 of this book.

Chapter 1
1. Louis XIV, *Mémoires for the Instruction of the Dauphin*, Paul Sonnino trans. and ed., Macmillian Free Press, New York (1970).
2. Moore (1903), section 59.

Chapter 2
1. For life histories, Bigelow, Campbell, and Pargetter (1990) have argued that the value of a life history is not given by the sum or average of momentary well-being over the course of that life history. The order in which good things happen matters.
2. Most of which has derived from the discussion in Parfit (1984), chapter 8.
3. Are there similar such cases where the preferences are generated by bias toward the near? This will depend on the rate at which you discount for temporal distance. If you discount exponentially (for example, where i is the intensity of a future pain and t is the temporal distance, by taking its significance to you now to be given by $i/2t$.), then your preferences will not change over time. If you do not then they will. See section 62 of Parfit (1984).
4. Future-bias generates many similar preferences, for example, when I wake up, knowing that I have a painful operation on a particular date, but not knowing whether it is in the past or future.
5. See Sidgwick (1907), pp. 381, 382.
6. See Rawls (1971), section 45.
7. See Bentham (1789), chapter 4. Though, to be honest, there is room for interpreting Bentham either way on this point.
8. Bergstrom (1966), p. 125.
9. Philosophers, following David Lewis, commonly refer to such triples as "centered worlds."
10. For any event, e, there are distinct properties *being past relative to e, being present relative to e, being future relative to e*. And that is just

the tip of the iceberg. There are also distinct properties *being in the distant past relative to e, being in the recent past relative to e,* etc.

11. This term has been used by several different philosophers in several different ways—sometimes to mean the block-universe picture, sometimes to mean the block-universe picture conjoined with the view that tensed properties are relational, sometimes to mean the block-universe picture conjoined with the view that tensed properties are relational conjoined with the view that objects persist over time in virtue of having distinct temporal parts wholly present at different times. So, for maximum precision, perhaps I should use a different term, but I find the one that suggests itself, "the uncentered block theory," unacceptably clumsy.

12. The metaphor is due to C. D. Broad (1923). Broad did not accept the view, but others have. See, for example, Schlesinger (1994), who calls it "hyper-kinesis."

13. This view may have origins in Aristotle. A contemporary version has been proposed by Tooley (1997).

14. Though many people have imagined this, I do not know of anyone who has endorsed it. Surprising, perhaps, because it seems uniquely well qualified to explain why the future matters and the past does not.

15. A view developed in McCall (1994).

16. The first and most famous presentist was Saint Augustine. For more up-to-date expositions of the view, see Bigelow (1996) and Zimmerman (1998).

Chapter 3

1. This is a term of art, and I introduce it guardedly. The advantages of using the word "present" in this context are that it supports both monadic and relational readings, and that, by doing so, I emphasize the structural similarities between this view and the analogous views in the metaphysics of time.

2. See Rosen (1990) and onwards.

3. The trickiness runs very deep. Indeed, it may be that there is no satisfactory way of answering all such questions without appealing to an intransitive "better than" relation. See Temkin (1996) pp. 175–210, and Norcross (1997) pp. 135–167.

4. The basic idea behind this piece of terminology is this: A deontic theory tells us what we ought to desire and do in a range of situations. An agent-relative deontic theory is one according to which whether or not an agent ought to favor one uncentered state of affairs over another depends in part on who he or she is. There are various ways of precisifying the basic idea. One way that I find use-

ful is to test to see whether a theory is agent-relative, try to state it in the following form:

For any agent A (A ought to favor uncentered states of affairs in which . . .)

If, for any accurate such statement of the theory, "A" appears twice between the parentheses, then you have an agent-relative theory. If not then you have an agent-neutral theory. This suggestion has origins in Nagel (1970), chapter 10.

5. It is not an accident that I find TGH's suffering so awful, of course. I find TGH's suffering so awful because she is my daughter. The point is that it is not her being my daughter that makes her suffering awful, to my eyes.

Chapter 4

1. To make this point cleanly, I am here assuming direct realism about perception. My perceptual object is the star, not a smudge of light or an array of sense data, but *the star*. Egocentric presentists do not need to be direct realists about perception, but the assumption helps to clarify the conceptual independence of presence and now-ness.

2. Many thanks to Benj Hellie for the form of this example.

3. Several of these examples are due to David Lewis. Variants of the objection have been addressed, in print, by Sider (2001) and Markosian (2004).

4. See Markosian (1993).

5. A lot has been written on this problem. A good starting point is Sider (2001), chapter 2, section 4.

6. Homer, *The Illiad*, book XXI, line 161.

7. Ibid., book XVI, line 283.

8. See Donnellan (1966) and Kripke (1977) for the classic discussion of examples of this kind.

9. Why? Recall the motivating idea behind egocentric presentism: Introspect in the right way and you will be confronted by a manifest truth—that a certain person's experiences are present. Some would say that you should take a revisionary view of that manifest truth, take it that what was really manifest was that a certain person's experiences are present-to-that-person. Egocentric presentists say you should take the manifest truth at face value. But of course, the precise nature of the manifest truth you should take at face value will depend on precisely who you are.

10. I have helped myself to something new here, the idea that it can be the case that from somebody's point of view a proposition is true.

But the move seems harmless enough. *From Mary's point of view* (the one with present experiences is female), so *from Mary's point of view* (P, the proposition that the one with present experiences is female, is true). This does not commit us to the controversial doctrine that propositional truth is a relative matter (see MacFarlane (2005)). It is not that P is true relative to Mary's point of view and false relative to CJH's point of view. P is false simpliciter. *From Mary's point of view* (P is true).

11. Note, if you find it helpful, that very similar options are available to monadic tensers as they try to make sense of past and future tensed utterances. To fix ideas, suppose that yesterday, in the midst of a Boston thunderstorm, Mary wrote on my blackboard, "It is now raining in Boston." Today is a fine day in Boston. What, then, do I make of what Mary said?

First, I might think her words express a false proposition:

Q   that it is now raining in Boston

But, though they say something false, they may be informative and they are certainly correctly written. Mary was correct in writing them, because she expressed a true proposition, because it was the case, as Mary spoke, that it was raining in Boston.

Second, I might think the words express a true proposition:

Q*   that it was raining in Boston

What proposition words express depends on whether their inscribing takes place now or in the past.

Third, I might think the words do not express any proposition at all. There is no sense in asking, "what do these words say?" You have to ask, "what did they say?" And in this case they said something true.

Chapter 5

1. This assumption is certainly implicit in many metaphysical debates. For example, there has been a long-running debate over whether modal realism (the view that, for every way our world might be, there is a world that is that way) supports moral nihilism (the view that all actions are morally permissible). See Adams (1974), Lewis (1986), section 2.6, and Heller (2003). All parties in the debate have assumed that, if modal realism really did support moral nihilism, this would count against it, in favor of some alternative metaphysical picture with less troubling implications.

2. Nagel (1986) p. 33.

3. I am deliberately equivocating here. Some reductionists believe people are bodies. Let them read "A's body" as "A." Others believe people are constituted by things that are not people—bodies— in the way that statues are constituted by things that are not statues—lumps of clay. Let them read "A's body" as "the body that constitutes A."

4. This is the broad argument of part III of Parfit (1984).

5. See Merricks (1998) and Zimmerman (1998).

6. Some variants of this view will have it that we are Cartesian egos. Others will have it that we are some other kind of thing (bodies, fusions of egos and bodies, etc.) but we go where our egos go.

7. The nature of the association is notoriously obscure. One way to construe it is to say that egos are located in space and time. Egos are literally speaking *inside* the bodies with which they are associated. Another way to construe it is to say that egos have experiences whose character is sensitive to the perceptual apparatus of the bodies with which they are associated.

8. Of course, Parfit never did offer it as an explanation of our judgments from inside and outside, so this is no criticism of him.

9. And the simple view fares no better here. Stipulate that it is a primitive, unanalyzable fact that Adam is the same person as Sili-Brain, and I will still judge, from the inside, that the three possibilities remain open.

10. The indeterminacy would not arise, of course, if the rules said "All *and only* balls that lie ahead of the path are in bounds" and "All *and only* balls that lie behind the path are out of bounds." Then it would be determinately true of my ball that it was neither in or out of bounds.

11. The technical use of this term was coined by Mark Johnston (1987). The idea is that the human being in Adam's vicinity, pre-operation, is physically just like the organism in Adam's vicinity pre-operation. They weigh the same, occupy the same region of space, have the same parts, and so forth. But the human being and organism have different persistence conditions. The organism survives the operation, because an organism can survive the loss of any one of its organs. The human being does not, because a human being cannot survive the loss of its brain.

12. Mark Johnston, who proposed a theory like this in Johnston (1989), explicitly welcomes this conclusion. But he is not trying to vindicate our judgments from the inside.

13. The explanation is in Nagel (1970), chapter 3, section 3.

Chapter 6

1. I am extremely grateful to Ninan for drawing my attention to this original idea. He develops it in "Persistence and the First-Person Perspective." I hope I do not misrepresent his final view.

2. One celebrated way to get such an ontology is to combine *perdurantism*, the view that persisting physical entities are four-dimensionally extended "worms," composed of short-lived temporal parts, with *unrestricted mereological summation*, the view that for any two physical entities there is an entity, their mereological sum, with them both as parts. This was the approach taken by David Lewis in his classic (1983) paper. But you can deny perdurantism and still think there are many temporarily co-extensive entities in the vicinity of a person.

3. This is my observation, I should emphasize, not Ninan's.

4. And you will be in good company. Several philosophers have suggested that, if two creatures share all my present parts, there will be an unknown fact of the matter about which of them I really am. Indeed, Eric Olson has used this to argue against the psychological approach to personal identity over time. See Olson (1997), chapter 5, section 5.

5. Philosophers of perception argue a good deal about what the objects of perception in ordinary and extraordinary cases are. Is what I see, when I see a rose, the rose itself, or something else, the very thing I see when I hallucinate a rose? And what, for that matter, is the very thing I see when I hallucinate a rose? Is it something in my mind? Is there nothing at all that I see? There is no pressing need for us to get embroiled in this argument here, to commit ourselves to any particular view of what perceptual objects are. But, to illustrate the basic idea behind this view of de se ignorance, I will talk as if a kind of direct realism were right: When I look at a rose, I have the rose as a perceptual object.

6. David Velleman has proposed a way of thinking about de se ignorance along the lines of ignorance concerning representations (what I have been calling linking ignorance) in Velleman (1996), though the details of his proposal are quite different.

7. If you are familiar with the existing philosophical literature on de se believing, you may wonder how my tweaked theory fits into it. Much of that literature has to do with the contents of de se beliefs. Should we characterize the contents of de se beliefs using *uncentered worlds* (see Perry (1979) and Stalnaker (1981)), or should we make use of more fine-grained things, *centered worlds* (see Lewis (1979))—where a centered world is an <uncentered world, person,

time> triple? Advocates of the Lewis approach say there there are certain de se beliefs whose content we cannot characterize with uncentered possible worlds. Advocates of the Perry/Stalnaker approach complain that distinct uncentered worlds may not represent distinct ways for the world to be. They are committed to characterizing contents using items that represent distinct ways for the world to be—*genuinely distinct possibilities.* I propose that we should indeed make use of items (worlds in which certain things are present) that are more fine-grained than uncentered worlds (thereby satisfying the Lewis concern), but these more fine-grained items nonetheless represent distinct ways for the world to be (thereby satisfying the Perry/Stalnaker concern).

8. Assuming, I remind you, that direct realists about perception are correct.

9. What exactly is a modally nonrigid referring term? It is usually defined as a term that "picks out different things at different possible worlds." The underlying idea is to think of terms as functions from worlds to things they contain. A modally rigid term has one thing in its range. A modally nonrigid term has more than one thing in its range.

10. This is the result of combining a perdurantist view of persistence over time with the view that, in some contexts, when I ask, "What do I have reason to do," "I" refers to a person stage, not a person. It is a popular view, explicit, for example, in Lewis (1983) and Sider (2001), and implicit in Parfit (1984) (for an argument that it is implicit in Parfit, see Brink (1997)).

11. See Perry (1976).

12. Again, Perry considers this explanation. But, to his credit, recognizes that it is less than satisfactory.

13. See Velleman (1996).

Chapter 7

1. Of course, in the inverted spectrum case too, the response will work only if I can be confident that there are *psychophysical bridging laws* that preclude qualia from dancing around unnoticed. David Chalmers argues for such laws in Chalmers (1996), chapter 7, but his arguments are not designed to convince the kind of skeptic we are considering here.

2. See chapters 5 and 6.

3. See chapter 3, section 3.4 in particular.

References

Adams, Robert (1974): "Theories of Actuality," *Noûs* 8, 211–31.

Bentham, Jeremy (1789): *An Introduction to the Principles of Morals and Legislation.*

Bergstrom, Lars (1966): *The Alternatives and Consequences of Actions,* Stockholm: Stockholm University Press.

Bigelow, John (1996): "Presentism and Properties," in *Philosophical Perspectives 10,* ed. James Tomberlin, Cambridge, MA: Blackwell Publishers.

Bigelow, J., J. Campbell, and R. Pargetter, (1990): "Death and Well-Being," *Pacific Philosophical Quarterly* 71, 119–140.

Brink, David (1997): "Rational Egoism and the Separateness of Persons," in *Reading Parfit,* ed. Johnathan Dancy, Oxford: Blackwell Publishers.

Broad, C. D. (1923): *Scientific Thought,* New York: Harcout, Brace and Co.

Chalmers, David (1996): *The Conscious Mind,* Oxford: Oxford University Press.

Donnellan, K. (1966): "Reference and Definite Descriptions," *Philosophical Review* 66, 377–388.

Heller, Mark (2003): "The Immorality of Modal Realism, or: How I Learned to Stop Worrying and Let the Children Drown," *Philosophical Studies* 114, 1–22.

Hume, David (1739): *A Treatise of Human Nature,* Oxford University Press (2000).

Johnston, Mark (1987): "Human Beings," *Journal of Philosophy* 84, 59–83.

Johnston, Mark (1989): "Relativism and the Self," in *Relativism, Interpretation and Confrontation,* ed. M. Krausz, Ilinois: University of Chicago Press.

Johnston, Mark (1997): "Human Concerns Without Superlative Selves," in *Reading Parfit,* ed. Jonathan Dancy, Oxford: Blackwell Publishers.

Kaplan, David (1989): "Demonstratives," in *Themes from Kaplan,* ed. Almog et al., Oxford: Oxford University Press.

Kripke, Saul (1977): "Speaker's Reference and Semantic Reference," *Midwest Studies in Philosophy II,* 255–277.

Kripke, Saul (1982): *Wittgenstein on Rules and Private Language,* Cambridge, MA: Harvard University Press.

Lewis, David (1979): "Attitudes De Dicto and De Se," in his *Philosophical Papers Volume I,* Oxford: Oxford University Press 1983.

Lewis, David (1983): "Survival and Identity," in his *Philosophical Papers Volume I,* Oxford: Oxford University Press.

Lewis, David, (1986): *On the Plurality of Worlds*, Oxford, Basil Blackwell.

Lewis, David (1989): "Dispositional Theories of Value," in his *Papers in Ethics and Social Philosophy*, Cambridge: Cambridge University Press (2000).

Macfarlane, John (2005): "Making Sense of Relative Truth," *Proceedings of the Aristotelian Society* 105, 321–339.

Markosian, Ned (1993): "How Fast Does Time Pass?" *Philosophy and Phenomenological Research* 53, 829–844.

Markosian, Ned (2004): "A Defense of Presentism," in *Oxford Studies in Metaphysics*, Vol. 1, ed. Dean Zimmerman, Oxford: Oxford University Press.

McCall, Storrs (1994): *A Model of the Universe*, New York: Oxford University Press.

Merricks, Trenton (1998): "There Are No Criteria of Identity Through Time," *Noûs* 32, 106–124.

Moore, George (1903): *Principia Ethica*, Cambridge: Cambridge University Press.

Nagel, Thomas (1970): *The Possibility of Altruism*, Princeton: Princeton University Press.

Nagel, Thomas (1986): *The View from Nowhere*, Oxford: Oxford University Press.

Ninan, Dilip (forthcoming): "Persistence and the First-Person Perspective," *The Philosophical Review*.

Norcross, Alistair (1997): "Comparing Harms: Headaches and Human Lives," *Philosophy and Public Affairs* 26, issue 2, 135–167.

Olson, Eric (1997): *The Human Animal, Personal Identity Without Psychology*, New York: Oxford University Press.

Parfit, Derek (1971): "Personal Identity," *The Philosophical Review*, vol. 80, no. 1, 3–27.

Parfit, Derek (1984): *Reasons and Persons*, Oxford: Oxford University Press.

Perry, John (1976): "The Unimportance of Identity," in his *Identity, Personal Identity and the Self*, Indianapolis: Hackett Publishing (2002).

Perry, John (1979): "The Problem of the Essential Indexical," *Noûs* 13, 3–21.

Rawls, John (1971): *A Theory of Justice*, Cambridge, MA: Harvard University Press.

Rosen, Gideon (1990): "Modal Fictionalism," *Mind* 99, 327–354.

Schlesinger, George (1994): *Timely Topics*, New York: St. Martins Press.

Sider, Theodore (2001): *Four Dimensionalism*, Oxford: Clarendon Press.

Sidgwick, Henry (1907): *The Methods of Ethics*, London: Macmillan.

Singer, Peter (1972): "Famine, Affluence and Morality," *Philosophy and Public Affairs*, vol. 1, no. 1, 229–243.

Stalnaker, Robert: "Indexical Belief," *Synthese* 49, 129–151.

Temkin, Larry (1996): "A Continuum Argument for Intransitivity," *Philosophy and Public Affairs* 25, no. 3, 175–210.

Thomson, Judith (2001): *Goodness and Advice*, Princeton: Princeton University Press.

Tooley, Michael (1997): *Time, Tense and Causation*, Oxford: Oxford University Press.

Unger, Peter (1990): *Identity, Consciousness and Value*, New York: Oxford University Press.

Unger, Peter (1996): *Living High and Letting Die: Our Illusion of Innocence*, Oxford: Oxford University Press.

Velleman, David (1996): "Self to Self," *The Philosophical Review* 105, 39–76.

Zimmerman, Dean (1998): "Criteria of Identity and the 'Identity Mystics'," *Erkenntnis* 48, 281–301.

Zimmerman, Dean (1998): "Temporary Intrinsics and Presentism," in *Metaphysics: The Big Questions*, eds. Peter van Inwagen and Dean Zimmerman, Malden, MA: Blackwell Publishers.

Index

access relations, 24–26, 28–29, 44–45
Adams, Robert, 57n1
agent-relative and agent-neutral
 deontic theories, 37, 100–101n4
anticipation, 86–89
assertion, 52–55

behavioral expression of inner states,
 xiv, 3–4
Bentham, Jeremy, 14
Bergstrom, Lars, 14
Bigelow, John, 99n1, 100n16
block universe theory, 15
branching and non-branching time,
 29
bridging laws, 93
Broad, C. D., 100n12

Cartesian egos, 63–64
Chalmers, David, 105n1
comfort, 1–5, 38–39
communication between egocentric
 presentists, 52–55, 101n10, 102n11
conflicts of interest, 6, 31–34, 37–40
consequentialism, 14–15
consciousness, xii–iii, 42–46
correctness conditions for belief and
 assertion, 53–54
cyclical time, 30

de se ignorance, 76–81
death, xiv–vi, 50–51, 86–89
direct realism about perception,
 101n1, 104n5 105n8
discontinuous time, 29–30
Donnellan, Keith, 101n8
dread, 86

egocentric hedonism, 1–8, 30–37
egocentric presentism, 8, 21–30,
 41–55, 81–98
epistemology of presence, 91–96

ersatz realism about the past and
 future, 15
eternalism, 15
evidence of presence, 91–94
extending indeterminate concepts,
 66–68

four dimensionalism, 15–17, 19

generalization: of agent-biased
 attitudes, 37–40; of egocentric
 hedonist attitudes, 5–6, 31–34;
 of time-biased attitudes, 12–13,
 17–18
greater good, xvii, 2–5, 9–11, 14, 18,
 31–37
growing block theory, 17

harmony, 2–8, 10–13, 18–19, 30–40
Heller, Mark, 102n1
Homer, xv, 50–51
Hume, David, xii–iii
humility, 49, 91, 96–98
hypertime, 47–48

identity over time. See personal
 identity over time
imagination, 43, 97
immaterial entities, 63
integrity, 97–98
intensity of sensation, 4, 35–36

Johnston, Mark, 103nn11–12

Kripke, Saul, xii, 70

Lewis, David, 102n1, 104n2, 104n7
linking questions, 76–81
Louis XIV, 1, 3

maps, 76–77
Markosian, Ned, 101nn3–4

111

CPSIA information can be obtained
at www.ICGtesting.com
Printed in the USA
BVHW03s2321190318
511024BV00001B/12/P

9 780691 178035